THIS IS THE PLACE

GLIMPSES OF WARREN COUNTY, IOWA

ELODIE OPSTAD

Introductory quote with permission from the Wall Street Journal, a division of Dow Jones

George Washington Carver quote courtesy of Simpson College:

Excerpt from *Beneath the Whispering Maples: The History of Simpson College,*by Dr. Joseph Walt; 1995 Simpson College Press, pg 150

Cover design and layout by Ellie Bockert Augsburger of CreativeDigitalStudios.com

Cover design assisted by Illustrated Historical Atlas of the State of Iowa byAndreas' Atlas Co., 1875

Library of Congress Cataloging-in-Publication Data

Name: Opstad, Elodie, 2024-author

Title: This is the place: Elodie Opstad

Identifiers

LCCN 2024917554 (print)

LC record available at https://lccn.loc.gov/2024917554

ISBN 979-8-218-48028-8 (print)

Subjects

LCSH: History/Iowa

LCGFT: Creative Non-Fiction–Essays

Classifications

LCC: F616-630 History–Iowa

BISAC: HIS036090 History–Iowa / POL046000 Political Science–Commentary/Opinion

Published by Elodie Opstad

Copyedit/Proofreading by Cari Dubiel

Distributed by Ingram Publisher Services

History shouldn't be taught as a memorization of dates or quotations, or as a huge survey. It is most appealing to anyone, but particularly the young, when you take a defined subject and bring it to life by telling the story.

DAVID MCCULLOUGH (1933-2022)
HISTORIAN AND AUTHOR

TABLE OF CONTENTS

INTRODUCTION

After writing a monthly column called "PastTimes" for the local printed newspaper, the publication was absorbed into a large conglomerate, lost its soul, and disappeared. However, the online *Indianola Independent-Advocate* soon launched with opportunity for a different style of writing. "The Unbroken Line of Pondering" commenced with two founding rules:

- Each piece would be less than four hundred words (increased to five hundred in March 2020)

- Last words of one piece would begin next month's piece, with those last words serving as the opening for the next, onward and onward in an unbroken line

After nine months, I found myself gravitating towards local history. Finding people and events lost to time felt like bringing buried treasure into the light. Just as fascinating were the insights, perspectives, and relevance to today. As a consequence, I added three guiding principles:

- Our digitized and searchable historical newspapers would serve as the primary resource for story ideas

- To avoid anyone living, I would steer clear of anything after the early 1920s

- Finding similarities with current events, my word choice, tone, and tenor could convey an inkling of attitude

I didn't know how long this writing could continue. Would I reach an unbreachable roadblock and fail to find new story idea? Would I lose interest? Would anyone be interested? Would I be dumped? Fortunately, nothing happened and I kept writing.

These glimpses of Warren County, with the exception of the first essay, were published from November 2019 through July 2024. They have been revised for consistency and clarification, which means some may now exceed five hundred words. Additionally, allusions to current events may have been smoothed because those happenings now reside in the past.

However, real and perceived inferences regarding political views and elections, immunizations, trusting our professionals, discrimination and acceptance, book banning, and school funding, remain intact. I accept full responsibility for misunderstandings, misconceptions, and errors.

While we all undoubtedly share broad swaths of general history, these glimpses focus on attitudes, actions, and experiences of individuals living through their time. How they managed, what they thought, and right, wrong, good, bad, with everything in-between, they made a difference. Sadly, these are the stories most often lost to time, making it important to support the work of your local historical society and anyone searching for the treasures where you live.

Thank you for purchasing this book because you are making a difference. All earnings will be donated to the Warren County Historical Society & Museum in Indianola, Iowa, because...

THIS IS THE PLACE.

ELODIE

WELCOMED BY
A NEW PLACE

"This Is The Place," Zebulon Hockett shouted to anyone seeking a better life. Arriving in 1848 aboard a groaning canvas-topped wagon pulled by a yoke of oxen, his wife Mary was likely pregnant with their first daughter. Zeb and Mary established the first general store and built the first frame house in what would become Indianola's downtown square.

It was August the following year when Paris P Henderson, Warren County's Organizing Sheriff, visited Zeb's vicinity with representatives from neighboring Polk and Madison counties. Tasked by the Iowa Legislature to locate eighty acres for a seat of justice, a representative from Jasper County was supposed to join their group but didn't make the trip.

On their way, perhaps in the shade of light timber with horses grazing nearby, Paris unwrapped his sandwich from a piece of newsprint. Spying an article about Indianola, Texas, he shared an idea and they collectively agreed it would be a good name for Warren County's seat of justice.

It's likely Paris P knew Zeb and Mary Hockett. As organizing sheriff, he knew all 649 Warren County souls and likely had a good idea where to locate the county's courthouse. While Sheriff Henderson lived in Ackworth, his hamlet wasn't in the center of the county and therefore unsuitable.

John M Laverty, another early settler, surveyed and platted the town. He placed an octagon-shaped public square in the center with blocks radiating outward divided into twenty-four equal-size lots. This platting constituted "Original Indianola."

Laverty submitted his straightforward and uniform design to Warren County's newly elected board in November 1849 and asked to be paid twelve-and-a-half cents per lot. They refused. Rather, he was paid two dollars a day while "necessarily employed." Today, the original plat resides in Volume X, page 138, at the County Recorder's Office.

While Zeb and Mary immediately purchased their lot, Jesse and Rebecca Liston weren't quick enough. Someone from outside the county bought their plot and forced the inconvenience of picking up their framed dwelling and moving it to an open and available lot on The Square's south side.

From this small beginning and following a bountiful harvest, a steady stream of emigrants arrived and settled. The influx meant more neighbors and "clubbing" opportunities. In those days, people worked together, which included traveling to Oskaloosa or Burlington for milling grain, gathering supplies, and collecting mail. Only the strongest made the journey with the cadre left behind taking care of hearth, home, and livestock.

This was a wild, woolly, and raw place, and Zeb Hockett's call to others wasn't their only welcome. An abandoned structure built of logs and aptly called the Naturalization House served as temporary housing for the newly arrived. Every mention of this dwelling uses the same words to describe its purpose: "It was called the Naturalization House because everyone who came to this city was compelled to live in it until they secured other quarters."

Returning To Our Roots and describing these early settler days seems a proper beginning for glimpsing through the windows of Warren County.

THE FIRST UNRAVELING

Returning To Our Roots includes the curiosity of finding someone named Moy Sing Bo buried in the Adams family plot at the Indianola Independent Order of Oddfellows (IOOF) Cemetery.

Moy Sing Bo owned a steam-heating laundry in Indianola from 1893-1909. Located south of The Square on Howard Street next to the old post office, in 1904 Moy's income was a stunning $3,500 ($100,000 today).

We know little about Moy except what's available in newspaper snippets where random bits of information deliver more questions than answers. Born in China sometime around 1864, he immigrated to India as a child and then to San Francisco in 1880 as a young man.

How Moy arrived to Davenport remains a mystery, but his obituary indicates being "taken into the (Davenport) home of the Reverend Rollins L Adams." The Adams had an adopted daughter Lida, a scant two years older than Moy. Lida and Moy undoubtedly knew each other before the good reverend joined the Des Moines Presbytery.

A wide-open Google search on "Moy Sing Bo" revealed he attended Grinnell College and lived in Newton, Iowa, during the 1891-1892 school year. Despite not graduating, this youthful man of Chinese descent later demonstrated great intelligence or an advanced education from somewhere far away.

In October 1893, the *Indianola-Times* reported Moy Sing Bo was looking for a location to establish a laundry. He was described as intelligent, a member of the Christian Endeavor Society (interdenominational youth society) and voted Republican.

Reverend Adams' wife passed away in 1897 and the following year he retired from the ministry. His last appointment was in Garden Grove, forty-seven miles south of Indianola, and sometime in 1899 the reverend and Lida moved to Indianola.

When the Adams arrived, Moy's laundry business was thriving as were his real estate investments in Indianola and Des Moines. He was well-known and respected. Not a feather was ruffled when he built at home next to the laundry for the reverend, Lida, and himself.

Sometime in the early 1900s, Moy Sing Bo installed a steam-heating plant next to his laundry using an idea already adopted by other Iowa towns. Sending steam heat through piping in an underground chase to his laundry, the post office next door, and up the street to The Square's southeast corner (Pageturners today), the below ground access remains intact today. This style of heating eliminated the dirt, smoke, and damage to merchandise other heating systems delivered.

In 1909, Moy served as the contractor for a 300-foot lateral sewer following the same route as the heating system. It was later conveyed to the city.

Reverend Adams died at ninety-five years in 1929 and his obituary proclaimed "the trumpets sounded at his entrance into Heaven." Lida never married and continued living with Moy Sing Bo in the house next to the laundry until her death in 1941. Moy died the following year and was described as a "man of modest income."

At the cemetery, a large granite family stone etched with the Adams name runs perpendicular to the individual gravestones. The good reverend is in the middle with Lida on one side and Moy on the other, but there's something that needs to be explained.

The wide-open Google search on Moy Sing Bo also found him on page seventy-eight of *The Sovereign Citizen*, by Dr Patrick Weil (University of Pennsylvania Press, 2012). Becoming a naturalized United States citizen on October 24th 1892 at Jasper County Courthouse in Newton, Iowa, Moy was denaturalized (lost citizenship) December 2nd 1913 in the same court. What caused the court to strip Moy's citizenship after twenty years? **Stay Tuned**.

THE FINAL UNRAVELING

Stay-Tuned are two words joined together asking for your continued attention. The term was coined during the days of dial-tuned radios without presets when finding the right station was a delicate task. The story of Indianola's Moy Sing Bo follows a similar path.

Moy arrived in the United States two years before enactment of the 1882 Chinese Exclusion Act, which not only banned the entry of this ethnic group but also denied citizenship to current residents.

For years the Chinese had been immigrating to the United States looking for a better life, and they were welcomed by mining, construction, and agriculture enterprises. However, their growing population created fear among West Coast whites until their presence was deemed a growing threat. This paranoia culminated in the 1882 Chinese Exclusion Act, with the legislation expiring after ten years (May 1892).

Moy Sing Bo became a naturalized citizen at Jasper County District Court in October 1892. He accomplished this feat during the in-between time after the 1882 exclusion act expired and before its replacement, the Geary Act, was enforced.

Taking classes at Grinnell College and living in Newton, Iowa, Moy likely had help from friends and sympathizers to obtain his citizenship during the interlude between legislative acts. While it could be perceived as an astute strategy or improper action, no one was watching.

When the Supreme Court upheld the Geary Act in May 1893, William H Schooley, owner of the *Indianola Advocate-Tribune*, found it regrettable and brutal because the new legislation added more restrictions. Every Chinese resident now had to carry a Certificate of Residence or risk incarceration. They also lost the right to go before a judge if arrested (habeas corpus), and interracial marriage was prohibited. If discovered, both husband and wife would be deported.

Neither Moy or Lida Adams married and the nature of their relationship remains a mystery. They lived together many years at the same address and were active in the community. Moy's work and travels reported in the newspapers as well as Lida's participation in women groups and community efforts. Their travel together was also reported, which wasn't any different or unusual from anyone else.

Jumping ahead to December 1913, a Jasper County District Court judge stripped Moy Sing Bo of his citizenship. Finding how this happened involved the State Historical Museum, Polk and Jasper County Courthouses, Grinnell College Libraries, and the National Archives in Washington DC.

Moy didn't lose his citizenship because of hatred or prejudice. It was the result of Mr AH Bode, Naturalization Examiner, doing his job. Examining records in Jasper County, perhaps specifically the gap between legislative acts, Moy's revocation of citizenship followed. AH Bode did the same examination in Polk County and all those naturalized citizens of Chinese descent lost their citizenship. Everyone losing citizenship in the same year for the same reason.

Extending citizenship to Chinese residents didn't happen until December 1943, the year following Moy's death. However, the first sentence of his obituary tells a story of acceptance: "Moy Sing Bo, Chinese naturalized resident of Indianola for more than 40 years…"

Riding his bike to and from work, Moy was a bona fide citizen of Indianola, which **Makes Your Heart Glad**.

HONORING
FORGOTTEN TREASURE

Make Your Heart Glad is a stirring string of words, which surprisingly didn't originate from a Bible passage, hymn, or poem. The phrase was written by Daniel Defoe in his sequel to *Robinson Crusoe*, with both books published in 1719.

The story of Robinson Crusoe begins with a stretch of youthful rebellion before he's marooned on an island north of Brazil and south of Barbados. Rebellion, repentance, and redemption follow this island exile responding to wickedly changing conditions without tools or amenities. Despite the novel's fragmented sentence structure held together by commas and semi-colons, it's a gripping story. Reading before bedtime will guarantee a slumber of swashbuckling dreams.

Daniel Defoe was a skilled literary hustler and published the *Life and Adventures of Robinson Crusoe* as a genuine and true experience written by an honest-to-goodness castaway. His fabrication met with immediate popularity, which continues today. Searching the online treasure trove of old Warren County newspapers, "Robinson Crusoe" served as a well-worn reference for other topics.

A June 15th 1882 *Advocate-Tribune* article running the length of the page found temperance warrior Francis E Willard mentioning Robinson Crusoe during her lecture at the Warren County courthouse. "Monarch of all he surveyed," she said, "until he found that footprint, not his own, in the sand."

Francis Willard was no ordinary person. At the time she was president of the National Woman's Christian Temperance Union (WCTU). This organization had become a large and influential political force with a strong stance on a variety of issues because of her long-term leadership.

Known as Frank to her friends, Willard's well-attended lecture shed a shining a light on Robinson Crusoe's diminished personal freedom after rescuing friend Friday from serving as dessert to a party of cannibals. Accompanying Friday's rescue came the responsibility of caring and nurturing for the poor man's body and soul while keeping him safe from danger and harm.

Miss Willard's reference to Robinson Crusoe meant Indianola voters needed to recognize and accept their responsibilities. Honoring hearth and home, state and family, they must vote to prohibit spirits and alcohol in next week's vote.

Prohibition triumphed at this statewide election and, since this popular vote aligned with legislative decisions during the past two consecutive sessions, Iowa's Constitution would now be amended. Prohibition of alcoholic beverages and spirits had finally prevailed.

However, powerful influences along Iowa's eastern border helped extinguish the flame of victory when Iowa's Supreme Court ruled the amending process unconstitutional. After years of temperance work, legislative hounding, and a supportive popular vote, the constitutional change was declared dead and gone.

Despite the setback, temperance work continued for years, and the people's voice finally triumphed with state-wide prohibition in 1916, followed by a national policy in 1920.

In December 1922, the *Lacona-Ledger* mentioned Robinson Crusoe, but not in reference to the evils of alcohol. Rather, the long-haired castaway might have experienced a more enjoyable and jazzy time during his exile with a newfangled invention—**The Radio**.

RADIOIST DAYS

The Radio might have been among the last innovations an ordinary person could understand and build themselves. Today we depend on enormous swaths of technology without a shred of knowledge or comprehension about their inner workings. As our understanding grows dimmer and dimmer, modernizations continue marching forward, bringing forth more nobler designs and enhanced capabilities.

Warren County newspapers first mentioned the radio in 1921, when it wasn't readily available. The *Indianola-Herald* reported Eldon Allen attended radio school in Illinois and the following year Edd Owens enrolled in the Ames Radio School of Instruction. He was interested in the device and considered owning one.

A flurry of radio happenings occurred in June 1922. Peoples Trust Bank installed a radiotelegraphy device (subsequently shortened to *radio*) in their lobby to broadcast the Omaha livestock and weather reports. The Kansas City grain report followed, with the broadcast ending after a summation of Chicago and Minneapolis markets.

That same month, the *Advocate-Tribune* reported the Empress Theatre would hold a radio demonstration before the picture show due to interest in the wireless transmission of sound. Jumping on the bandwagon, the Warren County Fair Board included among their amusements a wireless station equipped with a large "magna-vox" (speaker).

In August, the *Lacona Ledger* reported a trio of young ladies were entertained by a radio concert in the Ralston home with music from Des Moines, Ames, New Jersey, Kalamazoo, and Oakley. This newsy tidbit also mentioned, "Ice cream and cake was served and a wonderful time was reported."

Gustavius (Gus) Tilden, editor and owner of the *Lacona-Ledger*, published a radio column. Sporting a jagged lightning bolt banner, the content was highly technical and well-suited to tinkerers. Tilden also published easy to understand articles with catchy names like "Sparks," "Short Flashes," and "Tips for Radioists." His weekly newspaper devoted half a page to radio information.

Born in 1854, Gus Tilden emigrated to Warren County in his mid-forties after working for the railroad and riding the rails. He witnessed the untamed wilderness become smooth and contoured cultivated fields. He beheld fledgling towns become genuine cities as advancements, like the telegraph and telephone forever changed lives.

Gustavius Tilden must have felt a sense of profound amazement when the radio arrived. This feeling for new technology hasn't changed. Each of us can look back and recall a **Gee Whiz** moment of wonderment.

A GEE WHIZ
KIND OF GUY

Gee Whiz is a wild-eyed expression for something new and exciting. First coined in 1876, this diluted oath (Jesus!) was spoken but rarely found its way into print. However, Melvin Cecil (MC) Randleman of Carlisle and his son Zouave must have liked something in the phrasing when they patented their double-z Gee Whizz washing machine in 1901.

Their model included a top-loading wooden tub on stout legs. Inside, two metal disks spaced a foot apart rotated in opposite directions upon turning the side crank. The disks had rough surfaces to scrape and loosen dirt. According to collector and washing machine historian Lee Maxwell of Eaton, Colorado, the Gee Whizz defied description with its "scrubbing, mashing, mauling, twisting, squeezing action." It horrifically mangled clothes.

MC Randleman was born in 1830 and served in the Mexican War before moving to the southeast corner of Warren County during early settler days. He was an infantry captain during the Civil War and retired early due to exhaustion and disease. Outliving two wives, his family of nine sons and three daughters generated substantial laundry. Gee Whizz!

There were countless washing machine designs, inventions, and patents during Randleman's time. Frederick Louis Maytag of Newton, Iowa patented a wooden tub with a top-mounted hand crank in 1905. His model included a pulley for attaching to an outside power source (tractor or windmill).

Most women couldn't afford these early models and kept to the old ways of using a scrub board, boiling water, plenty of soap, hard work, and sweat. From a resource-altering perspective, washing machines, even those like the Gee Whizz, significantly impacted women. Spending less time on the labors of laundry, housewives could spend more time pursuing more creative endeavors. The washing machine was an empowering innovation.

Captain MC Randleman's curiosity and interest didn't end with the Gee Whizz. He patented a double-tined hay fork and a pig pen to prevent sows from squashing their young. His penchant for modern improvements included running telegraph wire a short mile to his house so his son, ten-year-old Charles Lincoln Randleman, could master tapping the transmitter key.

As a respected farmer, stockman, and early settler, the *Advocate-Tribune* occasionally published Randleman's thoughts on farming. In 1884, following three years of poor corn yields, his words remain worthy today: "Would recommend diligent work, applied in the right place and time. Trust in Providence, but be sure to **Keep Your Powder Dry**."

GOING ROGUE

Keep Your Powder Dry is a reminder to stay calm and carry on while remaining prepared to fight another day. Unfortunately, the advice wasn't followed by M Henry Money, owner of the *Weekly-Banner*, after President Lincoln's April 15th 1865 assassination. This terrible loss and vicious act shocked the world when it occurred less than a week after General Lee's surrender to Grant at Appomattox.

Losing the President immediately after the war left people angry, uncertain, and frightened. It was reported vile-talking traitors and conspirators remained among the victorious and righteous. It was in this setting that Editor Money struck the match to rekindle embers of hatred and panic, which undoubtedly increased readership and sales. His April 20th issue detailing Lincoln's assassination also reported a local woman giving thanks after four years of praying for the president's death.

A week later, a gaggle of ladies converged at this disloyal woman's home, forcing Jane Patterson into the street where she was made to carry a flag while recanting her evil ways. Jane's instigators followed closely behind, intimidating and ridiculing the poor woman.

In next week's issue, the *Weekly-Banner* published local physician Dr William Ball declared "it was a good thing Lincoln was killed," and that others were making similar remarks. Editor Money suggested violence could eliminate the unclean among us.

The good doctor's angry rebuttal in the May 11th issue included a threat, which set the stage for Money's well-crafted response: "If any bush-whacking, horse-thieving, mail-robbing fraternity of traitorous Democrats comes looking for him, they'd find a six-inch Colt revolver primed and ready to cheerfully deliver its contents to any copperhead (Democratic sympathizer) that visits with a belligerent intention."

In the same issue, the *Weekly-Banner* expressed its disapproval for mob scenes but questioned if Jane Patterson's clothes were truly torn and her daughter actually harmed during the recent hailstorm of womanly wrath. In Money's opinion, Indianola's finest and most upstanding ladies were only displaying a spontaneous and honorable show of grief.

The May 18th edition included Money's response to a lengthy column in the *Des Moines Iowa-Statemen*, an opposing Democratic newspaper. It was their opinion journalistic encouragement was linked to Indianola's recent violence. Editor Money reacted in characteristic style. Proclaiming the Des Moines editor as "a man of large bowels," he recommended "two anti-bilious pills followed by a cold-water injection with application of a mustard plaster to the affected area."

The same issue also questioned Jane Patterson's health and marriage, and called Dr Ball a "malignant type" of copperhead. Additionally, Editor Money declared violations of law and order, bloody riots, resistance, and disgraces in our country were most often instigated by Democrats.

Dr William Ball, an early settler and resident for twenty-three years, left Indianola to establish a medical practice in Arkansas. Upon his 1881 death, the good doctor's remains returned here for burial. On the other hand, M Henry Money, an Indianola resident of four years, sold the *Weekly-Banner* and departed in 1866 to publish a newspaper in Greene County, where his vicious vitriol followed.

Be Still My Heart, going rogue without truth or consequences hasn't changed a lick.

MISTREATMENTS

Be Still My Heart is an expression of overwhelming excitement accompanied by heart palpitations and high-strung nerves. Thankfully, remedies like Celerina were available.

Produced by the Rio Chemical Company of St. Louis, Missouri, Celerina sold for one dollar a bottle. It was heavily used by Dr Edward N Fishblatt, an itinerant physician visiting countless communities in the Middle West. Declaring to have dispensed a thousand bottles, the good doctor claimed having excellent results with Celerina in cases of sexual debility and nervous disorders.

Edward Fishblatt received his medical degree in 1865 from New York's Eclectic School of Medicine, which promoted homeopathic remedies while shunning blood-letting and leeches. In a time without antibiotics, he became highly specialized in the diagnosis and treatment of chancroids and ulcerative conditions resulting from syphilis and other venereal diseases.

Writing, publishing, and lecturing on the diagnosis and treatment of these afflictions, he recommended applying nitric acid, sulfuric acid, or a hot iron to all infected areas. It was essential to destroy all diseased tissue, regardless of future function, to avoid continued infection.

Dr Fishblatt drifted through Ohio and Wisconsin before entering Iowa's eastern border and moving inland. Adding Indianola to his repertoire in the early 1880s, he wasn't the only visiting physician but perhaps the most exuberant. Full-length newspaper columns extolling his virtues, devotion, immense practice, and guaranteed cures appeared weekly for months before the good doctor's arrival. His wife Mary might have been the powerhouse behind the planning and promotional push.

In 1885, the Fishblatts left Burlington, Iowa, where they had been living, and moved to the Minneapolis-St. Paul area due to their daughter Flora's condition.

When the *St Paul-Globe* newspaper reported Flora had been cured through the power of prayer, her parents became involved in faith healing. Feeling strongly about persons with similar afflictions, they turned their home into a private asylum.

Life was good until Mrs Mary Fishblatt died in 1894. Flora followed two years later while a resident at the School for the Feeble-minded and Colony for Epileptics in Faribault, Minnesota.

In 1898, the *St Paul-Globe* reported Edward Fishblatt had become a physical wreck unable to care for himself while addicted to drugs and alcohol. Taken to the county poorhouse in a dilapidated horse cart, he died at fifty years from his demons and distress.

The doctor's addiction and Celerina may have been related. In 1915, the *American Journal of Medicine* analyzed the acclaimed tonic and found a 42% alcohol level hidden under an aromatic infusion of plant oils (viburnum, celery, lady slipper, and prickly ash).

Years prior to the doctor's downward demise, the *St. Paul-Globe* published favorite quotes from their most prominent citizens and Dr Fishblatt was among them. Adding a missing part and modernizing phrasing, it predicted the good doctor's ill-fated demise: "It is by no means a fact that death is not the **Worst Evil** when it comes to alleviating those worn out with suffering."

CHARACTER COUNTS

Over a hundred years ago, the *Indianola Advocate-Tribune* reported the **Worst Evil** comes from those who are deceivers and backbiters—persons attacking the character of another.

Delving into the definition and substance of "Character," the word has an evolving history. Originating in early Greek culture, it meant an engraved mark or imprint on the soul. Over centuries it grew to define the sum total of a person's qualities and, with the addition of moral implications, made character count and very important.

"Character" remains a fairly popular word. It sits around 650 on the list of 5,000 most frequently used words (wordfrequency.info) with marriage, cancer, and responsibility falling hundreds of positions lower. Used thousands of times in Indianola newspapers between 1870-1920, and then rarely encountered before and after, the span of time exactly coincides with the Iowa Women Suffrage Movement.

Iowa made several good-hearted early attempts to give women full voting rights and they all failed. The fundamental persistent reason, aptly discussed and hotly debated, concerned a woman's character. Many men feared women didn't possess the intelligence, ability, and stamina for endeavors outside hearth and home. Additionally, bestowing women with full voting rights would lead to an irrevocable loss of feminine characteristics and render permanent damage to the sanctity of domestic life. Their character simply wasn't strong enough.

William H Schooley, publisher of the Republican *Indianola Advocate-Tribune* for twenty-five years (1877-1902), espoused this view, as did others.

However, with the passage of years and softening of attitudes, Clint L Price, owner of the newspaper after Schooley retired, published a fresh perspective in May 1916 from Mrs June Hamilton-Rhodes. As a relatively new Indianola resident, she explained her experience as a practicing California voter left her neither unsexed or unnerved by the obligation.

"The home has come to mean more than the house and lot upon which it stands," Hamilton-Rhodes explained. No longer isolated and independent as in early pioneer days, it included "the street on which the home stands, the community, of which it is part, and the state where it belongs." With home industries becoming community industries and eight million women working outside the home, she surmised, "We can no longer make the sharp dividing line that separates home and community."

June Hamilton-Rhodes was more than a wife, homemaker, and opinion writer. She taught physical culture to the women of Simpson College from 1912-1917, and her lessons extended beyond sports and exercise. She taught proper nourishment, good digestion, and required young women to use their entire lung capacity rather than old types of breathing. This five-foot blonde dynamo fought against bent shoulders, faulty carriages, crooked spines, and flat feet while cultivating proud, determined, and confident women.

However, remembering the battle women fought a hundred years ago and seeing too many old men hold powerful public offices for too many years, equality in representation **Falls Flat**.

A PANDEMIC
OF CONFLICTS

Warren County didn't **Fall Flat** or otherwise fail, flop, or flounder in caring for their poor, despite the Civil War's trauma and hardships. On July 31st 1862, more than a year after the war started and three years before it ended, our county board of supervisors published a notice in the *Weekly Indianola Visitor* stating they were gathering proposals to build a poorhouse.

On the front page of this same issue was a speech given by President Lincoln declaring that the South's rebellion against a perfect Union was taking time and more troops were needed. An adjacent column touted resolutions from both Republican and Democratic parties praising the valor of our soldiers and expressing gratitude for their service.

Turning to page three, an order from the War Department obligated Iowa to fill the ranks of five more infantry regiments. In the lower section of the opposite page, a solemn scene in Corinth, Mississippi where Iowa boys slept in fresh graves was poetically described.

During these pain-filled times, soldier letters detailing suffering and misery were regularly published amid pleas to help their families back home. Family farms lay in ruin throughout a divided United States during this never-before-encountered difficult time.

Despite the overwhelming pandemic of conflicts, Warren County moved forward to address the needs of the afflicted and destitute. It was only going to get worse.

At the time, Iowa's State Code placed responsibility for "Settlement and Support of the Poor" squarely on the shoulders of the county and consequently on the board of supervisors. However, they could delegate decisions to township trustees. This created a process steeped in personal bias, lacking in expertise and consistency, and without a central point of coordination.

In 1871, Warren County built a poorhouse on one hundred and twenty acres ($10/acre). Five years later, Superintendent Robert Zarley reported housing thirteen inmates between two and eighty years with everyone in good health. Residents were categorized as paupers, afflicted, crippled, old, needy, insane, and deformed.

The monthly report also listed assets. At the time, the county farm owned seven horses, thirty-eight head of cattle and one hundred hogs, along with plows, cultivators, hay rakes, forks, and hoes. Inmates worked the land, doing what they could to plant and harvest what they needed. Surplus corn, wheat, potatoes, butter, eggs, cattle, and hogs went to town to be sold. Meals consisted of coffee, tea, molasses, bread, butter, meat, potatoes, chicken, and eggs.

A local physician received a stipend for providing medical care, and the poor farm's cemetery accepted the departed. County poor funds reimbursed Reverend Sheets $4.75 for Bibles and two dollars was regularly approved to haul unfortunates to the county farm.

Apart from residing at the farm, township trustees could authorize payment for home assistance. Depending on the level of care, reimbursement seemed to fall between two dollars a week and four dollars a month. In 1876, poor funds paid twenty-five dollars to send five children by train to relatives in Missouri and thirty-five dollars sent a "cripple" to meet friends in West Virginia.

With publication of names and intimate details in the newspapers, **Privacy** held a wholly different meaning compared to today.

REVISITING
THE FAMILY CIRCLE

The essence of **Privacy** is to be unbothered and free from surveillance or intrusion. Today, we relate privacy to our personal health information and online activities. In early settler days, privacy meant the security and sanctity of the family circle.

When Warren County was a wilderness, the family circle was defined a close-knit sphere of family and friends providing support to one other to survive hard times, unforeseen circumstances, and catastrophes. This idea was firmly embraced and routinely called into action long before *Family Circle* became the name of a women's magazine.

In February 1865, the *Indianola Weekly Banner* published an ominous opinion piece entitled "Double Your Diligence." It was professed that, with the Civil War's impending closure, all of its wartime arousals and tendencies for corruption, crime, and wrongdoings would leave the battlefield and wiggle their way into communities. Everyone needed to help protect the family circle against imminent infestation. Ministers were asked to save the youth and guard all points of society. School teachers were counseled to "gird their loins like men" while facing their responsibilities.

Next to this two-column discourse was a sliver of newsworthy advice urging husbands and fathers to expand the intellect of their wives and daughters. Womenfolk should be allowed to read newspapers, not just fashion literature. Menfolk needed to guide their feminine family followers into becoming better conversationalists.

In May 1871, the *Indianola Journal* published another glimpse into minds of the times with a commentary on strong-willed women. This kind of woman was described as berating others while parading in unclean petticoats and dirty stockings. They pursued their own desires rather than home responsibilities and laid a path of destruction inside their family circle and any they could influence.

Conversely, good and reverent women possessed a cultivated intellect, pure heart, honest impulses, and maintained a dedicated duty to home, which was their God-given direction. Alongside this long-winded diatribe was a short piece debating if women should speak at meetings because this was very much an unsettled issue.

As a new century dawned, women began using an array of modern conveniences like the washing machine, vacuum sweeper, and electric refrigerator. While home responsibilities became faster and easier, expectations inside the family circle remained resolutely rooted in tradition.

In 1900, native Iowan Mrs Carrie Chapman Catt became President of the National Woman Suffrage Association. Her husband George voiced approval for her work when he said, "Carrie was a good housekeeper and cook, despite her absorbing interest in affairs outside the family circle."

In January 2020, *Family Circle* magazine ceased publication after almost ninety years and it was bad timing. With the COVID catastrophe calling for isolation, the idea of a family circle had returned and was being firmly embraced. While this modern calamity called for mitigation strategies like PPE (personal protection equipment) and social distancing, the tactics and goals were similar to those in early settler days—keeping a sphere of family and friends safe from harm.

However, going forward and **Coming Full Circle**, women still need to keep pushing for equality. We aren't there.

LOOKING FOR
A LOFTIER FUTURE

Coming Full Circle is an expression about returning to where you started...
It would be fair to think countless circling experiences over generations would
improve humankind's ability to listen, understand, and find tolerance. However, the
fight and fury surrounding the science of COVID and its kinship to Charles
Darwin's evolutionary theory rupturing the ramparts of Christian beliefs indicates
humankind prefers to keep circling.

The Origin of the Species, first published in 1859, didn't detonate an immediate
battle between religion and science. It remained silent and simmering until after the
Civil War.

In October 1870, the *Warren County Leader* mentioned the vigorous
controversy surrounding Darwin's tenets of natural selection, survival of the fittest,
and the beginnings of life. While this storm continued gathering, the idea of
spontaneous creation remained secure and unharmed without a chink in its armor.

In 1874, the *Indianola Journal* printed an opinion attributing the destruction of
Christian faith and beliefs to modern worldliness, pleasure seeking, and fast living.
Darwin's theory, taught by "unbelieving scientists," was considered only a minor
factor on the road to an evil and corrupt life.

The absurdities associated with Darwin's ideas continued finding a path into
print long past the naturalist's death in 1882, and there was no safe zone for
divergent opinions. This was a classic culture war. A person of true Christian faith
couldn't believe in evolution—not one little bit.

During Simpson College's 1884 graduation, Henry Livingston Loft's oration,
entitled "The Warfare of Science," entered the battlefield between steadfast faith

and sinful science. Reflecting on Copernicus and Galileo, Mr Loft attributed disbelief in their discoveries as originating from the most conservative elements of human nature. This outspoken student envisioned a loftier future where evolutionary theory and creationism could walk hand-in-hand. The *Advocate-Tribune* disagreed but found Loft's work well-written and demonstrating good training in its delivery.

Five years later, Simpson College dedicated a new science hall (Wallace) for the study of physics, mineralogy, and chemistry with room for a museum. Botany was the only life science mentioned. At the dedication and following two hymns, keynote speaker Reverend Bristol addressed the audience. Stressing the importance of basing our entire Christian civilization on divine intervention, he concluded by advising everyone not to ignore God as the "higher science of eternal life."

Henry Livingston Loft graduated, read for the law in Cherokee, Iowa, fathered ten children with one woman, and was considered a man of good habits and character. He was likely disappointed in the 1925 Scopes Monkey Trial after a jury of Baptists and Methodists found teacher John T Scopes guilty of violating Tennessee's anti-evolution law. Evolution and creationism weren't even close to living alongside each other when Mr Loft died in 1936 at seventy-nine years.

Speeding forward to 1981, the *New York Times* reported Iowa schoolteachers as intimidated by the evolution versus creationism controversy. They simply avoided both topics.

In 2017, Iowa House File 480 would have required Iowa teachers to include creationism in the teaching of evolution. The bill died in committee, but there's no immunity from another recurrence or even worser legislative regressions.

Keep vigilant on all fronts, much like the days when we waited for a COVID **Vaccine**.

ANXIOUS
FOR A VACCINE

Vaccine was a word frequently read, heard, and referenced as the world awaited a remedy against the ravages of COVID. Rooted in Latin and coined in 1798, the word refers to cows and the fluid Edward Jenner withdrew from the festering sores of diseased animals. Then, using a sharp point, he crudely scratched and embedded living virus into a nine-year-old boy, which left the lad with a scar and lifelong immunity to smallpox.

This fearful and dreaded disease spread like a grassfire, producing ugly disfiguring sores and carrying a 30% death rate. While "vaccine" originally referred to cows, its roots evaporated as meaning and definition expanded to include any artificially induced immunity.

While smallpox was the first scourge to have a successful vaccine, it took time to produce sufficient quantities. In 1870, Dr Henry A Martin of Boston became the first American to import tried-and-true animal exudate from the pus pockets of French cows. Arriving on ivory darts and glass squares, the good doctor inoculated his young fat and healthy cattle herd. After pustules appeared, Dr Martin dipped his small ivory quills into the oozing discharge to inoculate unsuspecting infants.

Everything worked perfectly and mass production commenced, which was time-consuming, expensive, and fairly disgusting work. Dr Martin ran the only vaccine farm in the United States for six years before competitors joined the effort. Vaccines against rabies, cholera, and typhoid quickly followed, with unregulated production in unprotected environments until passage of the Biologics Control Act in 1902.

When the smallpox vaccine became available, it didn't immediately grab everyone's attention in Warren County. While Indianola newspapers periodically reported snippets regarding its effectiveness and purity, they also printed unfortunate urban-legend-type happenings about rotten vaccines in distant places.

It was an 1881 smallpox epidemic in Chicago, Illinois following the rails to St Louis and infecting five Keokuk medical students along the way that changed minds. Too close for comfort, Warren County residents pursued inoculation at a vigorous trot.

Summerset reported having enough vaccine to relieve anxiety and concern, while Bevington's weekly buzz was "How did your vaccination take?" Everyone wanted a set of scratch marks followed by a fluid-filled blister leading to a scar for instant recognition of inoculation and immunity.

During the 1881 outbreak, the *Indianola-Herald* printed a home remedy to thwart the disease. Grinding foxglove (digitalis) with sulfate zinc (white vitriol) and mixing with water with a tad bit of sugar would strangle fever and restore the equilibrium.

Darby's Prophylactic Fluid was also advertised as the great germ destroyer. This glowing purple concoction eradicated smallpox, prevented diphtheria, and cured scarlet fever. Perfectly harmless, internally and externally, it could be used as a gargle, body wash, or household disinfectant. This all-encompassing fluid was also popular in brothels to hinder venereal disease.

In 1980, smallpox was declared globally eradicated after a two-decade World Health Organization (WHO) initiative. It took the entire world working in partnership and collaboration to annihilate this **Greatest Enemy**.

HAYSEED TRUISMS

According to JW Bruce, the **Greatest Enemy** was fear, which never won a battle and robbed health by keeping a person ignorant and far away from life's great lessons. This long-time Palmyra resident was an on-site local correspondent for the *Advocate-Tribune* from 1902-1914, with a byline of Hayseed.

Other towns like Wick and Milo reported their events in a factual manner but Hayseed used every opportunity to springboard into deeper thinking. Reporting that Eliza Halterman gave a swarm of bees to a neighbor prompted a keen observation: "Bees work for others and board themselves, house rent is all they ask."

In the same article, Bruce used 458 words to explain how outgrowing the brightness and originality of youthful thinking dulls the mind to fixed ideas with too little moisture. "Maturity, a much-abused term," he espoused. Immediately following his truism was a description of Mrs Alf Kelley's black rooster Jim seen wandering three-quarters of a mile down the road to the south and the same distance west.

James Wilson Bruce was educated but unimpressed by diplomas and credentials. He advised removing children from any institution should they exhibit tendencies outside the broadest definition of human kindness. As a lifelong learner, he treasured his library but didn't focus on only reading. It was important to return to the woods and open spaces, doing like the old Quakers in keeping periods of silence: "Meditating with your better self serves to make you alive and keep you that way."

Growing up when Warren County was a wilderness, JW Bruce (Hayseed) reported that children shouldn't be tamed or they'd fail to accomplish much. "Life is an easy flowing stream, if you let it flow," he said. "It's damming it up that causes the mischief."

After serving in the Civil War, this philosophizing farmer and correspondent returned home to plow unbroken ground. Raising a variety of crops, he sent rail cars of fattened cattle and hogs to Chicago and returned with fresh young stock.

Married and fathering eight children, Bruce found time to observe the small, contemplate the large, and stylishly share his assessments and appraisals without dithering or posturing:

- "Rev Holmes of Indianola preached, and attendance was above the ordinary and gave good attention."

- "Mrs Claud Morris and her father went to Wyoming to brush away the cares of life and see the country."

- "WB Schooler expressed (to his family) his desire for an automobile. There was silence in the camp and a look that told of a future."

- "Mrs Jane Pyle is battling with rheumatism and can't let go of her troubles."

- "No news this week, all busy, it's seed time. All are directed in their various channels, work all day and go to bed early, and sleep the unbroken slumber that puts silence to all dreams."

It's individuals like JW Bruce you want to resurrect. Filled to overflowing with unimaginable experiences and a mind exceeding the ordinary, he could us help find the right path or rightly lead us **To The Woodshed**.

MOBILIZING MINDS

To The Woodshed is a polite way of describing privately administered punishment with a giver and a receiver. In 1893, the *Advocate-Tribune* recommended using green elm wood on the backsides of boys who balked or developed unfavorable traits.

Vigilantes are different. They constitute a self-appointed group delivering punishment without reason, legal authority, or due process. Warren County experienced this style of frontier justice in 1848 when sixty men from here and neighboring counties forced the horse-rustling Reeves family to leave their home by leading them across the border into Missouri. Despite a negative connotation today, vigilantes held a certain appeal during the first World War.

When the United States entered the war in April 1917, Herbert Hoover was named our nation's Food Administration Director. Tasked with managing the entire food supply at home and for our fighting troops, his responsibilities included increasing crop and food production.

With a youthful beginning in Iowa, Director Hoover knew housewives ruled hearth and home. They held the power and influence to lead loved ones to meatless Tuesdays, wheatless Wednesday, and porkless Saturdays, with everyday conservation of sugar and fat.

Another idea of his was to organize a group of writers called "The Vigilantes" to weaponize wordsmithing in the direction of inspiring patriotism and self-sacrifice. Articles and poems written by The Vigilantes were distributed to newspapers across the county as a way to align hearts and muster minds towards wartime goals.

These literary works, published by the *Lacona Ledger, Advocate Tribune, Indianola Herald,* and *New Virginian,* were akin to Facebook and Twitter (X). Their messaging created targeted reactions and unified thinking, especially upon the death of a loved one:

> "Now this is the letter I write to him
> While my heart is sick with dread
> You are just where you should be, my son
> Standing staunch, where your duty led"

Hoover also implemented a pledge card campaign, setting a goal for 80% of households to join his food conservation army. A signed pledge card visible in the front window showed support for our boys in the trenches while shaming uncommitted neighbors. Warren County didn't meet the goal but "Hooverizing" became a national rallying cry and transitional verb.

Food was a factor in winning the war, and every county nominated a local volunteer food administrator. William Buxton Jr served Warren County with food rule reminders published weekly by the *Indianola Herald* and *Advocate-Tribune*:

> "You are unpatriotic if you have in your home more than one-
> half sack of flour. All flour and sugar found in violation of the
> law will be confiscated. Food will win the war. Save the scraps."

Today's vigilantes rally around social media. After claiming God and country for their side, any thought for worthy discussion is lost. However, before feasting on a gloriously delicious idea, consider context, and accuracy. Avoid nibbling on rotten fruit because **You Are What You Eat**.

RESTORING BITTERSWEET HISTORY

While the proverbial saying **You Are What You Eat** didn't surface until the 1930s, the idea of digestion controlling health and well-being became important around 1880. People were gravitating towards a more sedentary lifestyle, with bloating, dyspepsia, and heartburn becoming persistent companions.

From 1880-1930, digestion was mentioned thousands of times in Indianola newspapers with advertisements and testimonials plugging the power for a vast array of remedies. Cures like Hood's Sarsaparilla, Castoria, Dr Pierce's Golden Medical Discovery, and even Wrigley's gum, hermetically sealed in wax-wrapped packages, touted their digestive effectiveness week after week, year after year.

This advertising frenzy also included herbal bitters, which already had a long history of alleviating stomach problems. Among these restoratives were Brown's Iron Bitters, Mishler's Herb Bitters, Electric Bitters, and Prickly Ash Bitters, which seemed a local favorite.

Prickly Ash Bitters claimed to purify the bowels, strengthen and regulate the liver, aid in digestion, promote vigor of vital organs, and improve a sluggish brain with snap, vim, and energy. Developed in the 1860s by Dr Benjamin Franklin Sherman of Chillicothe, Missouri, the 22% alcohol-based concoction paired bitter barks with the numbing properties of the prickly ash bush. The recommended dose was a wineglassful after breakfast and half that amount before bedtime.

Dr Benjamin Sherman didn't live to experience the popularity of his compound. In 1875, he stopped at Shank's drugstore outside Macon, Missouri, with his friend Samuel Parker. They knew the proprietor kept a private bottle in the backroom. While all three men took a draught, Sherman and Parker tipped the bottle too many times. Leaving the store, they didn't get a hundred paces before falling down dead. While the bottle held whisky, it was also tainted by hydrocyanic acid, a deadly poison.

Meyer Brothers of St. Louis purchased the rights to Dr Sherman's compound, which they manufactured and heavily promoted to pharmacists as a business builder. Any druggist purchasing six dozen bottles received six months of paid advertisements in their local newspaper.

David W Husted, pioneer druggist on the north side of The Square, became a special agent for Prickly Ash Bitters. In 1899, he advertised the elixir week after week, month after month, in the *Advocate-Tribune*. Sometimes eight testimonials dotted the printed page alongside the paid advertisement from Meyer Brothers.

Prickly Ash Bitters bit the dust in 1916 when the Food and Drug Act declared its claims to restore and renew as reckless, false, and fraudulent. Meyer Brothers paid a ten-dollar fine and court costs.

However, Prickly Ash Bitters didn't fade away. It was resurrected by Boot Hill Distillery of Dodge City, Kansas, with appropriate substitutions for ingredients unfit for human consumption. Selling today for twenty-five dollars a bottle, the elixir enhances designer cocktails or can be sipped neat as a bittersweet liquor. According to its new maker, this American-style amaro delivers "complex hints of mint and citrus…followed by a slight numbing across the tongue."

Prickly Ash Bitters weathered the rages of time and found **Better Times**.

FINDING FAMILY

After the first great world war ended in 1917, an economic retreat followed and made finding **Better Times** difficult for Iowa farmers. Those returning from World War I and desiring a country life found little opportunity with the cost of land exceeding what it could produce.

The Canadian government, experienced in offering virgin prairie at low prices to those with stout hearts and strong hands, capitalized on the situation. Wanting to feed themselves and the world, they knew Middle West farmers came best equipped to tame their northern prairies. Like a fine racehorse born and bred for a singular purpose, Midwesterners had the know-how and stamina for turning prairie grass into cultivated fields. They also possessed the moral characteristics for becoming all-star Canadian citizens.

Warren County residents had been immigrating to Saskatchewan since the early 1900s, when Indianola's real estate mogul Harry Hopper began selling Canadian land. After Hopper's tenure, the Canadian government planted an agent in Des Moines offering discounted train excursions every first and third Tuesday. Warren County residents joined this ongoing exodus, populating towns like Milestone, Weyburn, Osage, and Yellow Grass. Visiting back and forth was routine and directionally dependent on the time of year with winters in Iowa and summers in Canada.

Since its 1857 inception, the *Indianola-Herald* dedicated significant space for community news from on-site correspondents. Their informational tidbits, often intensely personal, were organized by towns we recognize (Lacona, Carlisle, Prole) and others less remembered (Wick, Cool, Silent Lane, Social Plains). In March 1915, they added a Canadian correspondent to their stable of contributors.

Without regard to distance and international boundaries, "Osage, Saskatchewan" found itself firmly planted among its Warren County brethren

(Norwalk, Indianola, Palmyra, Milo, etc.). Keeping pace with the same newsy format, this northern enclave reported their weekly events:

- "Roy Erb was returning to Iowa for a visit."

- "Wilbur Hall's youngest had been sick."

- "Sid McBee's horse was cut by wire."

The newsy observations from this faraway northern enclave where treasured family members lived lessened distance and brought comfort.

The *Lacona Ledger* and *New Virginian* regularly published paid advertisements and articles about Canada's amazing possibilities, and the Canadian government paid for advertisements in Edwin Meredith's *Successful Farming* publication. At first these paid enticements bragged about crop size and yields, but in 1922 they began targeting women.

A beautiful and stylish housewife looking down a lush hillside where her menfolk harvested a flawless field said more than words. Canadian land was flat, fertile, and selling for fifteen to thirty dollars per acre. Yielding twenty to forty bushels of wheat per acre, this rich and bountiful land was surrounded by top-notch neighbors, churches, and schools.

However, Canada was also where, during a harsh and deeply cold winter night, Floyd Kellar smothered twenty hogs and eight milk cows after closing the barn door too tight. It was where seeing a ground squirrel meant spring was surely near. It was where the land needed to be worked in April for cutting grain in August. Yet despite its difficulties and challenges, this far northern region had an advantage—everyone knew cooler days killed germs.

Remembering this connection and following our roots, we surely have a thriving **Sister City** somewhere in Saskatchewan.

POWER OF THE PRESS

Sister City was a term used in early Indianola newspapers to either compare our superiority or highlight the incompetence of our neighbors. With Creston, Knoxville, Chariton, Pleasantville and Grinnell mentioned, Winterset was the most frequently referenced.

In April 1890, William H Schooley, accomplished lawyer, owner of the *Advocate-Tribune*, and strongly opinionated, published a news piece about sister city Winterset's upcoming vote restricting the freedom of their town cow. While the referendum failed, it ignited a burning flame of stewing and strategizing in Schooley's mind. Exactly one year later, he launched a campaign wielding the full power of his newspaper to alter the town cow's freedom in Indianola.

It's important to understand the town cow wasn't a single animal. In 1890, Indianola had 432 cows residing inside its incorporated perimeter without laws or ordinances to restrict their nomadic lifestyle. Forcing gates open and destroying shrubs, gardens, and fruit trees, while reeking of filth and leaving pie-shaped deposits, the town cow brought mishaps and mayhem.

When Schooley initiated his bovine battle in 1891, roughly 230 people owned 375 cows inside Indianola's city limits. While reduced from the previous year, it remained an impressive number.

On April 23rd 1891, the *Advocate-Tribune* reported visitors to Indianola walking to the depot to catch their train home encountered a herd of forty-three animals sauntering down the street. Schooley ranted, "A blind man with a bad cold couldn't miss it. Not one of them invested in property here."

Publisher Schooley continued pushing an aggressive pen using every opportunity to turn opinion against bovine freedom. There was support from Mayor Paris P Henderson, who pressed the issue during council meetings. City Auditor Hodson changed his stance after saving his children from being gored. Edd

Olive said he'd rather build a low ornamental fence around his property than an unsightly barricade against invasion.

In a four-line April 30th cheeky commentary, Schooley reported a number of children had been chased by cows but children were plentiful and it was important to maintain the town cow's liberty.

The May 14th edition of the *Advocate-Tribune* informed readers that petitions restricting bovine freedom had been presented to the city council. In the same issue, Schooley couldn't stop himself from inserting "The town cow must go" as a single line item wherever space allowed.

The town cow was a city council agenda item in June, and Schooley printed the opinion of every elected official. An adjacent news item reported Winterset's attempt to shoot a town cow, which left the animal intact but accidentally injured a citizen.

After crafting new ordinance language, Mayor Henderson hoped it would meet public approval in the upcoming November vote. Beforehand, Schooley reported the town cow deposited an early ballot on an unwary pedestrian who "put his foot in it."

The town cow lost its freedom that November with 2,314 voting to restrain stock and 1,402 against. Bovine freedom became, in Schooley's words, "A thing of the past, a scrap of profane history, a **Reminiscence.**"

TT TREASURE

We are fortunate for the writings of Thomas T Anderson, who passionately pursued **Reminiscence** in resurrecting the forgotten and memorable. Thomas T and brother James owned the *Indianola-Herald* from 1886-1910 and claimed their publication actually started in 1857, when the first hand-powered printing press arrived in Indianola.

Gifted in crafting images and conveying sentiments, TT Anderson published recollections from others and some of his own. These include four articles regarding his Civil War experience. Written over several months, the first recalled his 1861 enlistment in the Union Army, which took four attempts because he wasn't eighteen years old. After finally joining and returning home to pack, his father blocked the doorway. He didn't want another son joining the war. Once past this well-intentioned and loving obstacle, who pursued him for the first mile on foot, Thomas T made it to Des Moines, but without a warm coat.

Bedding down that cold August night atop the stagecoach, it was a miserable journey to Kellogg, which was the nearest railroad station fifty miles to the northwest. Recognizing the sound of chattering teeth, a beefy lieutenant pulled young Anderson inside his chinchilla coat. Held in a fatherly embrace, Thomas T never forgot the misery of that night nor the comfort and closeness of a complete stranger.

His second reminiscence dealt with punishment rather than glory during a hot April day in New Madrid, Missouri. Removing his woolen coat while on duty was an infraction in the eyes of Colonel Washington Elliott. Forced to walk around a tree for twelve hours without food or water, almost thirty others joined TT in disciplinary consequences that day.

Thomas T admitted harboring considerable resentment against his commanding officer until visiting him years later. Retelling his forced walk story,

Colonel Elliot explained that punishment was applied without thought of rank to ensure the 2nd Cavalry remained the best in service. Replacing resentment with love and forgiveness after all those years, TT Anderson was grateful for his conversion when the Colonel died two years later.

The third article was a tribute to Findley, oldest of the seven Anderson boys. He died during the Battle of Shiloh after taking a bullet near the heart. Left with only a mind's image of his brother's existence, Thomas T wrote this third reminiscence on the 39th anniversary of Samuel Findley Anderson's death.

Amazingly, Thomas and Findley were together at Benton Barracks in St. Louis before Shiloh's carnage. Talking non-stop until morning's bugle call, TT declared those long-ago conversations provided him with everlasting inspirational influence.

His fourth and final reminiscence reached way back to boyhood days, when Thomas and brother James drove their ox team, Duke and Dime, to Spray's Mill in Summerset. At the mill, they commenced bickering with schoolmate Samuel Ferrell, which caused stop-n-go fighting all the way home.

Anderson didn't see Ferrell again until his cavalry unit arrived by steamboat to Cairo, Missouri, where troops reported for assignment. Landing on a damp raw-edged evening, TT recognized Ferrell and realized, "Something great was coming into our lives, sweeping the foolishness of boyhood aside and transforming us into earnest men."

Rekindling their friendship, the boys became quite **Homesick**.

FOLLOWING
FAIRLY GOOD ODDS

Homesick is defined as a longing for home and family with a heartfelt desire for the familiar and accustomed. This kind of longing sounds like COVID isolation, except for experiencing the mirror image of too much time at home.

During World War I, letters from our boys in the trenches were regularly published in Warren County newspapers and homesickness was sometimes mentioned. In July 1918, Private Edison Polson wrote from somewhere in France about receiving twenty letters and several photos. After carefully examining the photos, young Polson confessed to being homesick. "Taking trips home in his dreams," he wrote, while also commenting, "Mother looked worried." Noticing a new tire on the left hind wheel of the sedan, he wondered what happened to the molded Goodyear.

A few months later, the *Indianola-Herald* ran a screaming headline, "2021 MEN READY WHEN UNCLE SAM NEEDS THEM." The coincidence in number of men matching the year of the writing caused careful scanning of the names for every duty-bound battle-ready soldier in Warren County. #1102 Oliver Fair Town of Milo sounded interesting. This young man not only survived the war but experienced a wondrous medical miracle later in life.

Oliver Fair Town was born in 1898 and named after his father, an early pioneer in White Breast township. Fair Town, as he was called, married after returning from the war, owned a barbershop, and helped friends and family on the farm.

Years later, this forever patriot helped the *Milo Motor* publish a photo and short biography of every local lad serving in World War II. Unbeknownst to Fair Town, the story of a life-saving mold was running alongside his everyday life and responsibilities.

The power of penicillin, discovered by Dr Alexander Fleming in 1928, wasn't an overnight success due to extraction, isolation, and purification problems. The first use of penicillin in the United States didn't occur until 1942, and the patient survived but used almost all of the nation's supply. Later that year, our country had enough penicillin, the first antibiotic, for only ten people. The problem triggered a worldwide search for a strain of the blue-green mold capable of surviving high production while maintaining potency.

In 1943, a woman employed at the Department of Agriculture laboratory in Peoria, Illinois, noticed a moldy cantaloupe at her neighborhood grocery store. The strain inhabiting the rind of her melon satisfied all requirements and its spores seeded a bountiful production for 2.3-million penicillin doses in time for the 1944 Normandy invasion.

On March 15, 1945, five months before the war ended, the United States federal government made penicillin available "through normal channels" to hospitals and pharmacies. At the end of that year, Oliver Fair Town was taken to Des Moines General Hospital with complications from the flu. The *Milo-Motor* reported he was "taking penicillin and showing great improvement."

Oliver Fair Town benefited from an injection of purified mold juice and lived another forty-three years. He left this world in 1988 at a whopping ninety-eight years.

For COVID, we had the benefits of Moderna, Pfizer, Johnson & Johnson, and AstraZeneca for a vaccine. Reflecting on history and playing the odds, trusting and following science makes a **Better Tomorrow**.

OUR GOOSE
WAS COOKED

Joseph Wachenheim, a saloon owner in Indianola, came to America from Germany looking for a **Better Tomorrow**. Arriving middle-aged and alone, he's listed as an Iowa State Capitol stonecutter in the 1870 census. He likely attended the first dedication the following year.

In 1874, Indianola's city council lowered the annual licensing fee for saloons from one thousand to five hundred dollars, which opened doors for this German Brewmeister. Old Joe took advantage of opportunity and opened a thirst parlor on The Square, despite the presence of a temperance group declaring, "We have no room for a beer hole in Indianola."

Late night fights and bad behavior dogged Old Joe's dramshop, fueling passions among temperance folk and especially the Honorable Lewis Todhunter. As a practicing attorney and former mayor, treasurer, and county auditor, Todhunter wasn't reluctant about using power and influence.

By the end of the year, the *Warren County-Tribune* suggested Todhunter deserved a pension from the county board of supervisors for serving as our guardian of public morals. Pursuing anything not meeting his standards had become a good living at county expense.

In April 1876, beer hall antics and temperance pressures pushed Indianola's city council to increase the annual saloon licensing fee from five hundred to three thousand dollars, but Old Joe wasn't thwarted. Asking a friend to approach Perry Crosswaite (pillar of temperance purity), he was able to purchase a sliver of property east of The Square (near Peterson Funeral Services). The location lay outside city limits with the Crosswaite and Todhunter families as Old Joe's neighbors.

Joseph Wachenheim, Brewmeister Supreme, built a 16x40 frame structure on that piece of ground and conducted a thriving business at his public house, which he named the Blue Goose. However, with neighbors irrevocably dedicated to prohibition, this co-existence was short-lived. Inside two months, a cadre of "snuff-pinching aristocrats" (Todhunter reference) extended Indianola's city limits and the Blue Goose's fate was cooked.

Troubles continued for Old Joe a week later when a gaggle of ruffians wouldn't leave his establishment after the beer was gone. Pushed out the door, they pursued re-entry and Joe emptied his revolver into their midst shooting one through the thigh and grazing another in the head.

By the end of July, Old Joe had multiple law enforcement infractions on file. After paying sixty dollars in fines and requesting a change of venue for three other charges, he sold the Blue Goose. It later became a cheese-making operation and then housed prize-winning chickens.

Old Joseph Wachenheim returned to Des Moines and made several forays into Warren County hoping to rekindle past glories of beer-making prosperity. However, stonecutting remained his primary occupation, which extended well past our statehouse's final 1884 dedication.

This was also the year Indianola implemented a new ordinance prohibiting the sale of all intoxicants. Todhunter tried extending the embargo to pharmacies but lost in court. Pharmacies continued selling intoxicants for medicinal purposes without a prescription.

Old Joe died in 1903 and is buried at Des Moines' Woodlawn Cemetery. His headstone is along the east side and very near the Hubbell mausoleum. The highly polished granite is pristine and unblemished with a simple chiseling of name and dates, as if **By His Own Hand**.

THEORY DIRECTS
AND ART PERFORMS

By His Own Hand aptly describes John M Folger, who came to Indianola in 1857 during early settler days. Young, newly married, and living in town, John made a living as a professional house and ornamental sign painter, which extended to carriages, buggies, and wagons. He also glazed and gilded with a specialty in wood graining. It took an artistic hand capable of fine detail to render the graining of oak or mahogany on a plain pine door.

In 1862, Folger enlisted and served as a hospital steward for the 34th Iowa Infantry during the Civil War. This Iowa regiment encountered more disease and suffering than any other. Losing his lower left jaw, John eventually received a pension of twelve dollars per month, which was significant and higher than most.

Returning home, John Folger resumed professional painting but now had several competitors. In addition to regularly running a paid newspaper advertisement, his work also received unsolicited praise. In 1886, the workmanship of his glazing and painting on the courthouse windows was mentioned in the newspaper as well as the wood graining on ordinary doors for several new homes.

Folger started a handwriting school before the war and classes resumed when he returned. While a two-line newspaper notice announced a new term, John devised a surefire method to set himself above and beyond his competitors. Selecting three respected citizens to examine before and after writing examples, they determined the most improved ladies and gents.

Submitting panelist and winning names to the newspaper, the notification looked official and not like a paid advertisement. It certainly eliminated doubt or hesitation about the school's value and credibility. Folger's writing school flourished for almost twenty-five years.

John Folger based his teaching on the Spencerian method of penmanship. Developed by Platt Rogers Spencer in 1840, the system uses nature's curves and ovals with ample flourishing. Tilted at a fifty-two-degree angle, the writing style shows a sense of movement, ease, and individuality. Spencerian penmanship became America's accepted handwriting method until the 1920s, when the typewriter replaced good writing skills.

While the endless repetitive drills of Spencerian penmanship appear prescriptive, mastery gives the hand the confidence to effortlessly and gracefully glide across the page without thinking. It was believed that only through continuous and tiresome repetitive practice could true artistry emerge. This freedom of personal expression resonated with Americans, and a simple statement in the lesson book's introduction embodies the concept: "Theory Directs and Art Performs."

During its heyday, "Spencerian" was a word describing any elegant movement. While cursive writing may have fallen by the wayside for now, the idea of freeing the mind through practice and mastery remains.

Today, giving a shout of "Nice Spencerian Style" could aptly describe a graceful curveball crossing home plate, the showy flourish of a brew-pour at West Hill, or a freakishly talented skateboarder gliding along Ashland Avenue.

Give it a try and don't worry, have confidence **In The Delivery**.

GOOD INTENTIONS PREVAIL

In The Delivery of Indianola's municipal services (electricity, sewer, water), there were bungles and missteps but always good intentions.

The decision for Indianola to build an electric power plant meant assuming debt for the first time and our dueling newspapers held clashing opinions. William H Schooley from the *Advocate-Tribune* called electricity an experiment in its infancy with safety concerns. The Anderson brothers at the *Indianola-Herald* desired leaving darkness and entering the illumination of a better tomorrow.

In March 1890, the citizens of Indianola voted in favor of electricity and debt. While erecting four hundred light poles infringed on several maple trees and provoked a little homeowner wrath, controversy remained minimal. On the evening of Saturday, September 13th, a great crowd gathered in darkness for electrification of The Square.

Marveling at what was accomplished, everyone toured the two-story power house to gaze upon the Edison system capable of igniting 1,500 electric lights at the same time. In the absence of meters to measure monthly usage, homeowners paid seventy-five cents apiece for the first three lights with the next three reduced to seventy cents.

In terms of tackling another utility, many Indianola homeowners used private wells for drinking water, which made sewage seepage into their water supply a real concern. In 1908, Indianola's city council developed an ordinance for sewage, which included building a city-wide system. Asking for public opinion, no one objected and a contract was "let" the following year to immediately connect the courthouse and jail. A gaggle of ladies were only too happy to establish a rotating schedule for keeping the courthouse public bathrooms clean and tidy.

City water followed a more bothersome path, despite good intentions. Troubles started in 1894 when Indianola's city council approved a plan developed by a citizen committee to build a water plant. Bonds were issued, which resulted in an unconstitutionally high debt load. Despite this escalating legal concern, the project moved forward.

It took until 1897 for Iowa's District Court to declare Indianola's indebtedness illegal with wrongful issuance of bonds. City water service was shut off, the plant engineer discharged, and ownership of the utility reverted to the bondholder.

The City of Indianola couldn't pay the rental fee, forcing a citizens' group to purchase the utility and make improvements in order to attract another buyer. During this time and years to follow, our city water remained largely unfit for drinking due to excessive amounts of minerals and a hazy yellow color.

Cascading problems included an insufficient water supply from the South River due to the absence of bedrock and shifting sand which hampered the pumps. Although another well was added, residents were regularly warned of night-time shutoffs to keep the standpipe filled for fire emergencies. The monthly water billing schedule was interesting: $2 for a small frame dwelling, $3 for large, $4 for soda fountains, $10 for schoolhouses with steam heat, $5 for tobacco manufacturers, and $5 for blacksmiths with two fires.

Eventually a 1915 newspaper article declared Indianola's utilities as "modern and beyond the experimental stage." It was pretty handy pushing a button for electric lights, flushing a stool, and turning a faucet for a glass of water.

Now was the time to move forward with a gas plant and street paving, because automobiles were **Becoming So Popular**.

SWEET INNOVATION
AND BITTER CHANGE

During the summer of 1900, it was easy to understand why the little Brownie camera was **Becoming So Popular** at Bert Osborne's pharmacy. This five-inch imitation leather cardboard box with nickel fittings sold for eighty cents and was simple to use. Even a child could take perfect pictures and Edwin Albert (Bert) Osborne's pharmacy provided a fully equipped darkroom for film processing at no extra charge.

The point-and-shoot Brownie designed by Frank Brownell at Eastman Kodak was revolutionary. Its innovative design took photography outside the studio, into the streets, and beyond into the surrounding countryside. Instead of painted backdrops, stiff postures, and frozen expressions, the art and craft of picture-taking was now accessible, affordable, and spontaneous. However, there were naysayers.

The *Advocate-Tribune* printed an article from the *Ladies Home Journal* claiming "Kodakers" were without manners or etiquette. Brownie owners departed from good breeding when they indiscriminately and promiscuously captured images of hapless victims. Fortunately, the little Brownie prevailed.

It should be noted Lydia Schooley was married to William, owner of the *Advocate-Tribune*, and she was a well-known photographer and business owner with a portrait studio.

Meanwhile, Bert Osborne's mind continued to wander and percolate while filling prescriptions and compounding medications. In January 1902, he purchased the failing Indianola Music Store and began selling a full line of instruments. Since the golden age of radio was twenty years into the future, owning instruments and making your own music was as normal as Spotify and YouTube today.

Later that summer, Bert installed a soda fountain for preparing perfect phosphate beverages of the highest quality. It was elegantly crafted of onyx stone with matching side columns holding fourteen porcelain syrup jars for making a myriad of bubbly concoctions. Electric lights and beveled mirrors adorned this modern structure, which was supported by an eight-foot oak refrigerator resting on a ten-foot marble base.

Osborne also began selling Columbia, Crescent, and Wasp bicycles, with Bert attracting considerable attention riding a motorized two-wheeler. However, in late November he suddenly sold his business. A notice in the *Indianola Herald* thanked everyone for their patronage and asked for their continued support of the Corner Drug Store.

The sudden sale of this thriving enterprise, which Bert Osborne surely treasured, was based on his young wife Daisy Mae (Talbot). Born in Indianola and married only three years, Daisy's health was rapidly declining and her physician advised moving west.

Leaving all they knew and held dear, Bert and Daisy departed for Los Alamos, Colorado. Many practitioners at the time suggested this arid mountain climate for treatment against consumption (tuberculosis). Historians estimate fully one-third of Colorado's early settlers arrived seeking relief and improvement from this dreaded disease. In 1900, pneumonia and tuberculosis were reported as the most prevalent cause of death in the United States.

Bert understood Daisy Mae's disease, its progression, and outcome. Osborne Pharmacy advertisements never guaranteed a cure for consumption but Boschee's German Syrup came recommended for a good night's rest.

Daisy Mae died in 1909 and returned home to Indianola for burial. Bert and his second wife visited Indianola with their son over the years, likely Kodaking to preserve spontaneous **Precious Moments**.

RIP-TARNATION
AND JOLLIFICATION!

In 1875, the *Warren County Record* printed a letter from early settler Andrew Hastie praising the value and benefit of several long-departed citizens but also calling attention to the living and breathing Joel Jacoby. Finding this letter 150 years later is a grand opportunity to bring forward the remarkable Joel Jacoby. It constitutes one of many **Precious Moments** in this unbroken line of pondering."

Trained as a cobbler, this resolute early pioneer from Philadelphia arrived to Warren County in 1855 with a young wife and commenced making shoes and boots. However, Joel Jacoby's keen mind soon applied itself to bettering himself and Indianola.

He started a lucrative livery and stable business and then sold farm equipment for a Des Moines dealer. This led to manufacturing his own wagons, carriages, and farm implements, which provided jobs to others. After helping bring the railroad to Indianola, he constructed Jacoby's Block on the north side of The Square. This came at a time when replacing frame storefronts with brick showed a thriving progressive community.

However, Joel Jacoby's worth as an upright person and leader with steadfast values is best exemplified by the "Fuss at the Fair" on October 16th 1868. The incident, reported by *Indianola Journal*, occurred eighteen days before a presidential election, the first since the end of the Civil War.

In this election Republican Ulysses S Grant was running against Democratic candidate Horatio Seymour and the great war's devastating impact and loss of life remained keenly felt. Reconciliation and tolerance seemed impossible with Democrats and Republicans battling over war debt, the cost of Reconstruction (infrastructure), and voting rights for African Americans.

By mid-October, Warren County had experienced countless torch-lighted Grant demonstrations with supporters in their recognizable military jackets and red pantaloons. Lending additional support, the Republican *Indianola-Journal* maintained a steady bombardment of innuendos and spiteful comments regarding their Democratic opposition. Tolerance and middle ground seemed lost as falsehoods kept anger and outrage fueled and simmering.

Rip-tarnation! Imagine a regiment of Republican Grant supporters and their wives entering the fairgrounds on that October evening after an inspiring rally. Approaching the gate as a loud and boisterous group, fair president Thomas Thompson, a steadfast Democrat from Kentucky with a broad-brimmed hat and long hair, decided they couldn't enter. A few of his rowdies tried shutting the gate and several heads got knocked before President Thompson ordered fair marshals to close the gate and send everybody home.

As threats escalated and big-time violence seemed imminent, Joel Jacoby, a recognized Democrat and the fair board's treasurer, stepped forward. He told the Republicans they could pass and offered to pay their admission.

Given the respect Joel Jacoby garnered, people calmed and the Republicans escorted their wives through the gate. The evening settled into a good time for all.

Jollification! Despite differences and diversity, **Community Spirit** prevailed.

HOME MADE PRIDE

In late October 1919, owner of the *Advocate-Tribune* Clint Price wrote about **Community Spirit** and what makes some "localities" more desirable than others. His article defined a contented people as "Taking an unselfish interest in the affairs of others while participating in worldly interests without smothering local traditions."

Editor Price's thinking wasn't random; it was calculated. He was soliciting support for a new property tax to build a memorial honoring Warren County soldiers and sailors from all wars. The proposed structure would take the form of a public hospital.

Despite every precinct voting the referendum down, Price and others pursued an alternate idea eight months later. Once again, community spirit lacked lift-off for a memorial hall and armory. The idea fizzled after several committee meetings.

Since Indianola's 1864 incorporation as a real bona fide city, community pride and responsibility had been leveraged to rally, influence, and sway. This included annual springtime mayoral proclamations requested homeowners and businesses to remove all ashes, garbage, manure, tree branches, tin cans, broken dishes and glassware, from their properties, backyards, and alleys. Encouraging community pride was also applied to shopping local, which included cigars.

In August 1900, long-time Des Moines resident Henry Hansch purchased the Indianola Cigar Factory because he'd fallen in love with small town living. The *Indianola-Herald* wrote this gentle German had forty years in the cigar-making business and was only asking for hometown support. He would deliver "good goods."

After two years, Henry remained at the helm of his one-man operation doing the stripping, filling, binding, rolling, and wrapping with little help. While it was his goal to keep small and local, satisfying a diverse range of hometown preferences remained a challenge.

The Anderson brothers at the *Indianola-Herald* periodically published cigar factory updates and Henry was always grateful. He merely desired more Indianola businessmen to smoke "home made" cigars rather than those from a foreign house (Des Moines).

This good quiet citizen sold the previous owner's blends, which included Jack's Best and Cut Dime (a nickel favorite), while adding a few of his own: Henry's Best, Key West, Fair Exchange, and American Perfecto. However, Henry hit a hometown homerun when he introduced The Pride of Iowa.

The Pride originated around the time his son August returned from cigar-making in Chicago. Together, father and son turned out stogies by the thousands alongside new blends like Little Pet and Tom Rush. However, The Pride remained a local favorite. After re-introducing the retired Cut Dime in early 1903, Henry died from a disease described as "displaying a cancerous nature" before the year's end.

The Indianola Cigar Factory continued with August making homemade stogies without the filth and dirt plaguing larger operations. Wrapping each and every seegar like his father, The Pride remained the local leader.

The Anderson boys at the *Indianola-Herald* continued promoting shopping local and reported smoking a cigar wrapped by Mr Hansch, "Thoughts grow brighter and **Troubles Pass Away**."

PURGING AND POLISHING

Troubles Pass Away when a man has a good wife and in 1857 the *Indianola Weekly-Advisor* had definite ideas on the subject. Their front-page article reported a good wife's first duty was to conform to her husband's circumstances, never her own.

In 1864, another front-page commentary reported a good wife creates a sanctuary and place of repose and keeps a sweet and gentle demeanor with good humor despite her husband's bad behavior.

Nothing changed in 1871 when the *Indianola-Journal* published yet another front-page article confirming the man as head of the household and asserting all good wives want it that way. Another snippet of information declared it was a husband's responsibility to educate his wife, desiring her identity to be absorbed into his.

In a search of Warren County digitized newspapers from 1857-1920, "good wife" had 464 hits compared to 153 for "good husband." With many "good wife" mentions in obituaries, women were also richly described as loving mothers and true friends.

Pondering the idea of word frequency, it wasn't a leap to wonder about the n-word in our old newspapers. This racial slur, the most offensive and inflammatory in the English language, came into use around 1755 and was always meant to be insulting and contemptuous. Checking frequency, there were 462 instances of the word in our newspapers—almost matching good wife.

Reflecting on tolerance and intolerance, an eloquent essay entitled "The New Tolerance" on the front page of the June 21st 1888 issue of the *Advocate-Tribune* remains timely. Written by Simpson College junior Mattie Stahl, she was born in 1861 at the start of the Civil War. Growing up after the war, the evolution of her thinking reflects its aftermath during reconstruction and reconciliation.

Mattie Stahl believed truth ultimately triumphs but the victor's story is one of fatigue and ongoing hardship. While opponents may be overcome, they remain unconvinced. It was Mattie's thinking that purging lingering beliefs took time and grinding relentless work over generations.

"Tolerance for the person, intolerance for the creed," she wrote, because remaining loyal to convictions, yet tolerant of the opposition, was important in order to keep moving forward. Mattie, even at her young adult age, already knew changing thinking to eliminate harmful institutions and stubborn traditions would always be difficult.

After graduation, Miss Mattie taught school before returning to Simpson College as Professor of the Latin Department. She was popular, respected and, giving a speech during 1903 commencement activities, told graduates to cling to their ideals, remain brimful of enthusiasm, and maintain a zest for intellectual learning.

Mattie Stahl resigned from her professorship the following year and married Randolph Beall of Mt Ayr. She became a good wife while maintaining her identity. In 1924 she was the first woman to join the board of trustees at Simpson College. Despite women achieving the vote four years prior, the board never considered adding a woman. Only doing so upon failing to meet accreditation requirements.

For Goodness Sake!

ABIDING
THE PASSAGE OF TIME

"For Goodness Sake," the *Lacona-Ledger* wrote in 1919 when Warren County farmers wanted to return to "Old Time." Springing ahead into daylight saving time from March through October was well and good during World War I but victory had been achieved, it was time to return to normal. While this shifting of time for seven months provided an extra hour at day's end, it was confusing roosters and milch cows. They didn't know the difference.

After the war, businessmen on the East coast advocated continuing daylight savings time. Among them was manufacturer Marcus A Marks of the New York-based National Daylight Savings Association. He claimed shifting time saved a million tons of coal for electric and gas lights, which caused eyestrain due to their glare. Moving time forward also lowered food expenses and provided an early evening hour for gardening. While these claims were never validated, repeated use created the illusion of something real and factual.

"Daylight savings is not popular," the *Lacona-Ledger* proclaimed. "Taking an hour from morning work and placing it at day's end was disarranging farm life. It created a nuisance."

Farmers in the corn belt couldn't abide by the hardship and began organizing a kind of country versus city rebellion. Henry A Wallace and his father supported the rural viewpoint inside the pages of their *Wallace's Farmer* publication. Local farm bureaus, like the one in Warren County, which formed during the war to organize and distribute food, became strong voices opposing daylight savings time and they applied pressure.

In March 1919, Iowa's General Assembly drafted a resolution to Congress requesting repeal of the "humbug law." Iowa fields needed the extra early morning hour to dry and farm help was using daylight savings as a reason to quit at six o'clock when summer light remained.

Petitions circulated and farm families, along with their livestock kept to sun time or old time. Coming to town on Friday night an hour later forced merchants and businesses to remain open until midnight while rural customers strolled and socialized.

The *Lacona-Ledger* kept the topic current and constant until, on June 27th 1919, Congress succumbed to the demands of Middle West farmers. An amendment repealing the daylight savings law was on its way to the president's desk. While President Wilson vetoed it twice, Congress prevailed by overriding his repeated reluctance. Time returned to its original setting on October 26th 1919, making daylight savings an individual state decision until the next world war.

Reflecting on the experience, Henry Wallace advised farmers to establish a strong organization at local, state, and national levels. With minds and hands busy in the field, they needed a strong voice at all legislative levels. Since the Federation of Farm Bureaus helped eliminate the foolishness of managing daylight, they seemed the perfect partner for the job.

Throughout this controversy, the earth, sun, and moon never wavered from keeping to their **Established Schedules**.

FOLLOWING THE HORSES

Established Schedules without change or alteration was outside true-to-life thinking when the Western Stage Company ran their mail delivery routes in the mid-1800s. At the time, stagecoach service was a step above a fast pony and before the iron horse's arrival.

The Western Stage Company is remembered for their Concord coaches seating nine persons drawn by six horse teams (think Wells Fargo). Their gritty tobacco-chewing drivers ruled the road wielding long reaching whips, although weather and road conditions actually reigned in terms of keeping to schedules.

A team of horses could travel five-to-eight miles per hour and cover ten-to-fifteen miles before they needed to be exchanged. Following the horses, livery stables soon expanded their amenities to include meals and overnight accommodations.

The Western Hotel at the southeast corner of Indianola's square might have been among the first to serve the traveling public. The Coffman House, Jacoby House, and City Hotel followed, with each establishment attached to a livery stable.

Stagecoach service in Indianola included southerly routes into Missouri through Osceola, Chariton, and Burlington, with an east-to-west route stopping in Knoxville, Pella, and Winterset, before continuing on a rugged path to Council Bluffs. Schedules and departure locations were regularly published in the newspapers.

Mail between Indianola and Des Moines arrived and departed on Mondays, Wednesdays, and Fridays, with eastern and western postal deliveries on Tuesdays, Thursdays, and Saturdays. James H Knox, owner of the *Indianola Weekly-Visitor*, complained about delays and omissions because it left him scrambling for news.

As the railroad inched closer, dissatisfaction with the Western Stage Company mounted, and competitors developed. Local entrepreneur Joel Jacoby started a thrice-weekly hack from Indianola to Des Moines on Tuesday, Thursday, and Saturday, leaving at six-thirty in the morning and returning at two o'clock in the afternoon.

After repeated complaints about eastern mail mess-ups, the team of Lothrop & Coffman started a competing service to Pella. Promising timeliness, one of their hacks was cut to pieces within a month. The *Weekly Indianola-Banner* reported it was the work of "some cowardly mean sneak who is desirous of assisting the Western Stage Company."

While the stagecoach provided entrepreneurial opportunities for stabling passengers and steeds, it was always about location. Halfway between Indianola and Osceola, a distance of thirteen miles, seemed perfect when Mrs Charity Rice of Ohio platted a corner of her hundred acres for the village of Madora. According to a County Auditor plat book, Charity's daughter-in-law Rachel Rice owned several downtown blocks, but neither of these Ohioans spent time here.

It wasn't long before the railroad upstaged the stagecoach and what was known as Madora lost its appeal. Interestingly, Charity named the town Madora, which morphed into Medora. Both spellings are connected to the Greek goddess Medea and constitute a girl's name meaning Ruler. What was Charity thinking?

Indianola newspapers used Madora and Medora interchangeably with both appearing on the same page. The discrepancy informally settled in 1885 when the *Indianola-Herald's* local correspondent declared, "Either will answer, Madora or Medora, but Medora is right."

He Was Wrong.

A SWASHBUCKLING TALE

"He Was Wrong," wrote Captain Charles King in his 1890 novel, *The Deserter*, a thrilling story of army life published by the *Advocate-Tribune* in eighteen weekly installments. Filling five columns or almost the entire page, a scattering of small pen and ink illustrations provided the only break in the action on the densely packed page.

In the late 1800s, serialized novels published by weekly newspapers delivered the walloping dose of romance, action, and adventure we get today from Netflix, Prime, Apple, and other favorites.

William H Schooley, owner of the *Advocate-Tribune*, published a steady stream of novels in slices. Among them were two by rock star Sir Henry Rider Haggard: *King Solomon's Mine* in 1887 and *Nada the Lily* in 1892. The latter boasted the novelty of an all-African cast and it is still available today via Amazon Audible for $7.99.

In the first installment of *Nada the Lily*, Mopo confesses to killing Chaka, the first Zulu king. Later, Nada, the most beautiful of Zulu maidens and Mopo's daughter, is killed. However, she's resurrected in the 15th installment when Mopo declares he's wrong. Nada-the-Lily wasn't the lifeless form in a pool of blood—it was someone else.

As the end of a serialized novel approached, the *Advocate-Tribune* began promoting the next suspenseful selection. These stories of adventure, action, and faraway places sold newspapers. Even more enticing to Schooley and other publishers was not having to typeset the action-packed pages. They arrived preprinted with the reverse side blank for inserting local news and advertisements.

These preprinted pages were called "Patent Insides" and came at nominal cost. Like Facebook today, they held advertisements around the edges promoting products like Hire's Root Beer (a great temperance drink) and Wadham's Axle Grease (because horses know the difference).

Patent insides became a lucrative business for a handful of companies and George Joselyn of Omaha had the foresight to purchase all competitors. Becoming the supreme leader of this business niche in the early 1900s, his company owned thirty-one plants. Printing standardized pages for twelve thousand newspapers, his business spanned twenty-five states.

These inserts had detractors. Graham & Baker at the *Indianola-Herald* declared this mode of operation as "Stale news from cheaply gotten up papers." Reading the *Des Moines Register* today about a surge of garage sales in Cincinnati could be construed as today's version of patent insides because it fills the page with nothingness.

But let's move forward and get lost in *The Foundered Galleon* by Weatherby Chesney and Alick Munro. Published in 1899 and released in page-covering action-packed installments: "Guthrie and the eight souls aboard the Eureka hadn't thought of sailing as dangerous or ominous...but now was the time for proving the truth or falsehood of their hopes...Wealth for all of them if Dr Tring was right, and if he was wrong—death!"

To Be Continued.

DON'T BUMP
YOUR HEAD!

"To Be Continued" ended the first installment of a three-part exposé published by the *Weekly Indianola-Visitor* in mid-April 1860. Wesley M White, Warren County's first elected county school superintendent, needed multiple issues to finish commenting on his fifty-one schoolhouses and their corresponding teachers:

- "Mr Green of Washington Township is wanting in energy and decision in the management of his school."

- "Mr Cleland of Indianola appears to be a gentleman with the good will of his students, but labors with more than one hundred pupils."

- "Mr Cook in Palmyra township was not in the best of humor owing to the congealing properties of weather and absence of fuel."

- "Mr Hall of Liberty township is poorly qualified for the business of teaching."

Superintendent White concluded his report by congratulating our school system's progress before launching into the issue of low salaries. "We can't attract eminent scholars," he declared. At the time, male teachers received $13.55 per week and females $4.49.

Even before publishing his observations, this eager-beaver school superintendent convened the first Warren County Teachers' Institute during Christmas week. The all-day sessions covered grammar, arithmetic, and reading, with intermittent prayers and singing. There was a penmanship discussion, with Superintendent White's "Capitals" deemed unsurpassable, and a debate about classroom governance.

While the Golden Rule was mentioned, Wesley White blew past the cliché saying he didn't believe in governing by authority and control. He favored bending behavior by studying and understanding pupil personalities. "Phrenology," he said, "would greatly aid in the treatment of individual cases."

This long-ago discussion regarding handling students and classroom governance continues today and is mindful of closing lines in the *Gloria Patri Doxology*: "As it was in the beginning, is now and ever shall be, world without end, Amen."

Superintendent White's mention of Phrenology, the study of reading head bumps, might have been the first mention of this pseudoscience in our newspapers. From 1860 forward, it gained in momentum and popularity. In April 1871, the topic was actually debated by Simpson Centenary College professors Carpenter and Grumbling.

Professor Grumbling taught chemistry, physics, mathematics, and German. He might have been the conservative voice to Professor George Carpenter's more liberal thinking. Carpenter taught literature, natural sciences, and maintained an all-consuming passion for nature's wonders and man's ingenuity for inventions—like the telephone.

Because Professor Carpenter admired Charles Darwin, Simpson's Board of Trustees branded him as having "a mind bent on speculations, which in many men would have been dangerous."

Meanwhile, itinerant phrenologists continued arriving in towns throughout Warren County well into the 1890s. Offering free lectures and examining members of the audience, these bump-feelers determined if couples were "mated or mismated." Their carnival-like performances likely destroyed any credibility Phrenology might have possessed.

However, the companion practice of Physiognomy, the study of assessing character and intent through facial expressions, didn't topple into obscurity. It lives and thrives today as the hot and growing industry of **Surveillance And Recognition**.

IT'S ONLY CUBAN ITCH

Surveillance And Recognition became controversial subjects in January 1901 when Thomas T Anderson's daughter Eva returned home after visiting Atlantic, Iowa, where smallpox was reported.

After Eva complained of a sore throat followed by fever and skin eruptions, their family physician deemed her medical condition suspicious and the entire Anderson household went into lockdown. With "Quarantined for Smallpox" placards surrounding their property, this co-owner and editor of the *Indianola-Herald* began working from home.

The scare didn't go unnoticed by William H Schooley of the competing *Advocate-Tribune*. He reported the Andersons' panicked reaction with a taunting headline, "Smallpox!!! Smallpox??? ---Oh Well Perhaps."

Schooley's two column commentary two weeks later entitled "Quarantine Nonsense" reported no one in the Anderson household contracted smallpox and neither did Eva's isolated friends. It should be noted Schooley was a trained lawyer and never studied medicine, while the Andersons were following physician advice and Iowa Board of Health guidelines.

The *Indianola-Herald* didn't respond to Schooley's baited barbs but kept reporting the whereabouts of isolated households in Warren County. They weren't hard to identify with their yellow and black quarantine flags flapping in the wind. During these times, health information wasn't private, it was openly displayed, shared, and reported.

At month's end, Iowa's bout of smallpox encompassed sixty counties and, like pandemics today, naysayers and rule-followers lived alongside with endless bickering.

In February, Schooley's newspaper published an Iowa Board of Health professional review for a Hamilton County physician. Despite experiencing 2,000 cases of smallpox over the past eighteen months, this physician declared their outbreak as a milder form of pox without the need to follow strict quarantine requirements. Claiming a diagnosis was as easy as knowing a jackass from a horse, he would lift a scab on a pustule and, seeing a dent or pit, declare it chicken pox. Finding a hard mound of flesh, he deduced smallpox.

Schooley maintained his skeptical attitude while reporting pox outbreaks and wasn't alone. Others questioned if Iowa's invasion had been the genuine variety or a lesser form called "Cuban-Itch." Many Iowa newspapers reported the doings and whereabouts of pustule-infected individuals going about their business claiming to have Cuban-Itch. When public health officials intervened, the diagnosis was always bona fide smallpox.

Warren County's invasion abated in early spring and the reprieve continued until mid-October when smallpox returned. Wearied by disease and just before Christmas, Hartford naysayers removed their quarantine cards and released the isolated after declaring their outbreak as Cuban-Itch. The following month, Hartford's local correspondent for the *Indianola Weekly-Herald* had nothing to report owing to a smallpox scare.

At the start of the new year and in light of Des Moines' swelling smallpox outbreak, Editor Schooley published an article declaring that our Capitol city needed to vigorously enforce strict quarantine requirements. There were pustule-infected people roaming the streets.

Did William H Schooley change his mind about Cuban-Itch and smallpox? It's possible. His newspaper's style of faithfully reporting exactly what he thought was never **Fair And Impartial**.

A TEAR-DOWN
FAMILY FEUD

In February 1876, **Fair And Impartial** wasn't on the minds of many in Warren County after the Tear-Down Church murders. The killings involved the Westfall and Howry families of Greenfield Township, who had been feuding for years over an unsettled accusation of theft.

Because legal proceedings never resolved their festering fissure, the clash between families continued growing. Entangling everyone in the township, from parishioners at the North River Church to the children in the schoolyard, they were anointed with the Tear-Down moniker.

A church meeting was called to reconcile the parties but the feuding families didn't arrive in a prayerful state of mind. They came liquored-up and well-supplied with guns, knives, clubs, and slingshots. Leaving the meeting at the same time, the families barely passed the church cemetery when a battle ensued. Within minutes, two Howry boys lay dead in the dirt. Their cousin died two days later after giving testimony that Benjamin Westfall stabbed him twice while standing and three times when he was on the ground.

The sheer violence of the altercation rocked Warren County and the sensational news spread to newspapers throughout Iowa, the Middle West states, and continued east to Scranton, Pennsylvania. With the unharmed Westfall combatants simmering and stewing in Indianola's jail, a congregation of inflamed minds representing Polk and Warren counties took action. They formed the North River Detective Association.

The *Indianola Weekly-Tribune* published the association's founding principles in a letter signed "Vigilante." Stating the Tear-Down Church murders would never have occurred if the laws of the land had been enforced, the North River Detective

Association declared they weren't being over-reactive or reckless. In fact, they were organized. With a thousand dollars in start-up funds, their charter of incorporation was on file in Polk and Warren counties with a list of officers. Their mission was to suppress crime and administer justice with offenders punished based on circumstances—not governing law.

Des Moines newspapers began reporting wild rumors and fake news about an imminent insurrection and impending violence brewing in Indianola to hang the Tear-Down murder culprits. The Westfall gang was moved to Fort Madison prison for safekeeping.

Wagering readership and livelihood, John A Everett, editor and owner of the *Indianola Warren-Record*, Warren County's only Republican newspaper, took an alternate and less electrifying approach. Publishing an article entitled "Mob Law," Editor Everett condemned Des Moines papers for their irresponsible publications of rumor and innuendo. There was no evidence or truth in what they were printing.

Deploring the murders, Everett believed: "Mob law would find no encouragement among better class communities…It is the less thoughtful class…and generally the excited rabble that executes the damnable heresy of mob law."

In the end, none of the knife-wielding Westfalls served prison time and a lighter form of family feuding continued in Greenfield Township with shenanigans, nasty exchanges, and legal actions. The North River Detective Association faded into obscurity or their actions went dark, and Warren County citizens listened to Editor Everett and remained a **Better Class Of Citizens**.

ALLOW HISTORY TO REPEAT ITSELF!

In February 1889, posters promoting Duncan Clark's Minstrel Show at Spray's Opera House horrified Indianola's **Better Class Of Citizens**. The vulgarity of the artwork caused two local ladies to circle The Square daubing red paint on areas of concern. However, defacing the posted notices likely brought greater attention to the fully-formed figures and increased ticket sales—especially the expensive 75¢ front row seats.

Unbeknownst to Henry Spray, owner of the opera house (south side of The Square), the Duncan Clark minstrels had a history of single nighttime performances followed by speedy exits to avoid jail time and fines. While advance newspaper advertisements described their Arabian Nights Show as gorgeous, superb, and entrancing, actual performances brought comments of fraudulent, obscene, rank, jadish, notorious, and risqué.

Indianola's performance was attended by men only and William Schooley, owner of the *Advocate-Tribune*, was rumored to be in the front row. His review described the minstrels as scantily clad in the same form-fitting costumes used by circus performers but their songs and actions were unqualifiedly lascivious. Schooley commented opera house owner Henry Spray was careless bringing the troupe to town but any crusade against him needed to end. Going forward, it was best for residents to support the opera house by attending events of genuine merit because the performance hall was doing poorly.

Henry Spray continued booking shows of all kinds—comedy, plays, and specialty groups showcasing mind-readers, magicians, and contortionists. It was almost impossible not to offend someone. Three years after the Duncan debacle, Indianola's chapter of the Women's Christian Temperance Union (WCTU) presented a petition to city council. They wanted an ordinance prohibiting indecent minstrel troupes from posting their bills.

The WCTU was a national organization initially created to defend temperance (alcohol abstinence) while advocating for prohibition (outlawing alcohol). After years of gathering members and power, their clout had grown to include national positions on women's suffrage, stricter naturalization laws, and ensuring the sanctity of the Sabbath.

The *Advocate-Tribune* reported the WCTU's request to city council on page two with an editor opinion on page three. William Schooley disagreed with passing an ordinance to cure a moral ill and wrote: "The question of decency is largely a matter of fashion, education, and opinion." He also mentioned nothing of indecent or immoral nature had occurred since an incident several years before—an obvious reference to he-who-shall-not-be-named Duncan Clark.

Clear heads prevailed at Indianola's council meeting when they deferred the WCTU's request to another committee, where it promptly disappeared into the bowels of city government.

Meanwhile, Duncan Clark and his minstrel show continued crisscrossing the country, incurring fines and creating havoc until September 12th 1900. Pulling into Mound, Illinois, their special railcar collided with switch engine No 128. Nine performers were instantly killed and three more died later. Duncan Clark survived. Many thought his immoral show finished and kaput but he re-built and toured another twenty years.

Contemplating today's clamoring to legislate everything from pronouns to bathrooms and from book banning to women's health, allowing matters to get lost inside the bowels of government doesn't sound **Too Awful**.

BUDDING BUSINESS
GOES BUST

Too Awful describes the life of Madalene, a nymph du pavé (prostitute) in a three-column tale written by James Maxfield and published by the *Indianola Weekly-Herald* over several weeks in May 1875. The story follows Madalene's depraved but penitent and spiritually pure life, ending with her death and a lesson from scripture: "Let him without sin cast the first stone."

Besides writing stories and poems with moral purpose, Dr James Maxfield maintained a thriving dental practice on the southwest corner of The Square. Born in Ohio and having to work at a young age to support his widowed mother, he had little opportunity for proper schooling. While never training at the Ohio College of Dental Surgery, Maxfield might have learned from a graduate. There were only two dentistry colleges in the entire country at the time.

After serving as a corporal in the Union Army, Maxfield emigrated to Warren County and spent considerable time selecting a bride. The *Indianola-Journal* admonished him for dawdling and getting fat from courting. He married Laura Noble in 1871 and they had four children, two of which survived infancy.

Dr Maxfield's advertisements mentioned his skills for painless operations through careful administration of nitrous oxide, plus the know-how for extracting, filling, and putting in teeth made of rubber, silver, gold, and platinum. The good doctor was tender—not rough. Serving on the first State Board of Dental Examiners, he later helped define Iowa's standards for care and licensure.

Apart from his profession and creative writing, Maxfield became an expert in the budding business of raising silkworms. His articles, published throughout Iowa, created considerable correspondence and responding to them became a burden.

In 1883, Maxfield started the June season with twenty thousand worms and fresh ideas about Iowa's silk culture, including its pecuniary or money-making advantages. Raising white Japanese silkworms, he discovered they tolerated Iowa's weather fluctuations and didn't require mulberry trees. Feeding his worms at six in the morning, noon, and seven at night, he calculated forty rods (660 feet) of Osage orange hedge could feed forty thousand worms.

After thirty days and five molts, the worms achieved enormous size before attaching themselves to branches and spinning cocoons. Since robins were major predators, he protected his squirm of worms with netting.

In early days, American silkworm cocoons were sent to France for unwinding the filaments and spinning them into silk thread. It wasn't long before the United States government began encouraging and subsidizing this component of the industry. Factories in Michigan and Pennsylvania eventually processed thousands of American cocoons.

However, the-times-they-were a-changing as fashion-mindedness became important and clothing evolved into ready-to-wear. It's unknown how long the good doctor raised worms, but before Maxfield's death at eighty-three years old in April 1919, he must have known about artificial silk. This inexpensive first-to-be-produced man-made fiber derived from reconstituted wood pulp was later given the name Rayon.

While raising American silkworms spiraled into obscurity, the healthy and vigorous hedges of Osage orange throughout Warren County remained **Horse High, Bull Strong, Pig Tight**.

THINK OF OTHERS—
BE A GOOD NEIGHBOR

The phrase **Horse High, Bull Strong, Pig Tight** combines all the right elements for conjuring the image of an impregnable farm fence. The phrase went viral in 1859, after being coined and published by Wisconsin's *River Falls-Journal*. Originally used in jest and sarcasm for defining an unattainable lawful fence, the expression today describes superior fencing materials of the highest quality.

In early pioneer days, farmers had little money for lumber and wire, which made planting a living fence their best option. In March 1868, the *Indianola Weekly-Visitor* mentioned John and Imle Eno had contracts to plant fourteen hundred Osage orange saplings. It was well-known "the boys," forty and thirty-eight years respectively, always delivered as promised.

Imle Eno's success in the hedge business, which included planting a hundred miles of Osage orange, is mentioned in the *1879 History of Warren County, Iowa*. However, these living partitions didn't meet the requirements and expectations of a lawful fence.

In 1871, Iowa's Supreme Court agreed with a lower court decision that farmers should only receive compensation for damages from trespassing animals if they had a lawful fence. This ruling meant Iowa's Code of Statutes was turning away from Common Law, which made owners responsible for their animals' transgressions with or without a fence. This easy-peasy way of settling disputes was no longer applicable.

"Nor in harmony with the genius of our institutions," wrote Iowa Supreme Court Justice William Miller before his closing remarks expressed what he really thought: "Were this question an open one, he would on constitutional grounds come to a different conclusion."

With the taming of Warren County, fencing out intruders to protect fields of wheat, corn, and oats became a farmer's burden. Adding to the turmoil, township trustees were the designated fence reviewers for settling disputes and assessing damages. Iowa's fence and herd laws were definitely works in progress.

After the iron horse arrived in Indianola, durable fencing materials became more readily available. In 1874, the *Warren County-Tribune* published the definition of a lawful fence to help farmers understand their responsibilities. Besides length and height requirements, there had to be three rails of good substantial material, on equally substantial posts, and wire (when used) substantially built. This lawful definition left substantial open ground for roaming interpretation.

Herd law continued progressing over decades with the courts interpreting gray areas and oddball situations. This included deciding who was responsible for damages when male animals trespassed and interfered with a neighbor's vulnerable breeding stock, and who paid damages for loose animals running amok on unimproved ground.

For one hundred and fifty years, Iowa's Supreme Court has been called upon to interpret and settle herd and fence transgressions. Unfortunately, it's never been good enough to follow simple thinking: Think of others—Be a good neighbor.

In 1995, the final words from Iowa Supreme Court Justice David Harris on yet another fencing situation showed pride and respect for this incessantly questioned and intensely interpreted section of Iowa Code when he said, "It is difficult to imagine a more **Deeply Rooted** Iowa statutory provision."

DISCOVERING
PLUCK & SPUNK

Silas Igo of Palmyra wrote an article for the *Advocate-Tribune* about the **Deeply Rooted** prejudice against the Aberdeen Angus in August 1906. It seems the breed encountered many obstacles when first introduced in the United States.

"To begin with," Igo wrote, "we had never been accustomed to the black color." At that time, shorthorn brown cattle garnered all focus and attention. However, the Angus had an important niggling feature—they were hornless. Injuries, maiming, and death were much more common among more temperamental horn-laden varieties.

Silas Igo started his Angus operation six years before penning his celebratory article about this noble highland breed but didn't introduce them into Warren County. That honor belongs to early pioneer William Noble.

Taking a chance on the Aberdeen Angus wasn't completely foreign to Mr Noble. Like the breed, he was bred, born, and raised in Scotland before immigrating to the United States. Farming first in Hardin County, he arrived in Warren County with his family in 1865 and permanently settled.

Years later, Noble visited his Scottish highland homeland, where he might have contemplated breeding these glossy black beauties. In the spring of 1884, he purchased three bulls, three cows, and four harmless heifers at a Kansas City auction.

Arriving at the Indianola train station, Noble paraded his newly acquired Aberdeen Angus herd around The Square, and they stood quietly to be examined. Their surprising appearance warranted several healthy-size paragraphs in both newspapers. The published accolades declared William Noble as intelligent, enterprising, and thrifty. Despite prejudice and obstacles, he above all others took the leap of faith to bring a new breed into Warren County.

William Noble trusted and believed in the big-eyed beasts and they delivered. People's minds changed on seeing the highest quality meat produced in the shortest amount of time at the greatest possible weight.

It's unknown if Silas Igo knew William Noble. Their lives surely overlapped despite a forty-year age difference. Silas, born in Palmyra, spent his boyhood fishing, snaring, schooling, and driving stock for his father. While successful as an Aberdeen Angus cattleman, his true calling emerged after serving as the auctioneer for a school box supper.

Taking a chance and trusting in faith and ability, if he could sell a lady's box lunch, he could sell cattle. After calling for an Indianola auction and another in Palmyra, there-go-Igo never looked back. Traveling nationwide, he sold more Aberdeen Angus in public auction than anyone anywhere.

Silas Igo died in 1955, after a long lived eighty-eight years. It's common for those with extended lives to have compressed obituaries because dying young and tragically warrants greater length and detail. However, snippets of his life are revealed in our online searchable newspapers (warrencounty.advantage-preservation.com).

Stumbling on individuals lost to time and discovering their pluck and spunk is akin to finding treasure. Understanding their character, drive, and daring to become our own locally grown **Best Of Breed** is more difficult. However, it may have been eloquently expressed in the closing lines of *Invictus*, a popular poem penned by William E Henley in 1875: "I am master of my fate; I am Captain of my soul."

BATTLING BAKING POWDERS LEAVES LADIES APOPLECTIC!

Finding **Best of Breed** among baking powders created a minefield for housewives when all baked goods were homemade. Before these life-changing powders became available, saleratus, a chalk-like chemical, provided the means to savor-the-rise without yeast.

In 1861, saleratus was available in paper packets at Indianola's Noble & Harrison's Country Drug Store. Four years later, Bishoprick's Baking Powder became available but wasn't easy-peasy. It required the same preparation as making a common pudding.

A decade later, Brick Grocery on West Main (Salem), where deliveries were free, offered both Tone Bros and Dr Price's baking powder. The Illinois-based Price powder was the first to use cream of tartar as a leavening agent and the good doctor made a fortune. Dr Price was soon battling New York's Hoagland Brothers and their cream of tartar-based Royal Baking Powder.

As the Price vs Royal conflict bubbled and percolated, smaller enterprises entered the field with products of questionable purity and unknown toxicity. The exceedingly high-rising profitable business of baking powder was occurring when our nation lacked food protection and truth-in-advertising laws.

In a paid August 1884 advertisement published by the *Advocate-Tribune*, Price accused Royal of having a product containing ammonia, dirt, lime, and potash. Royal countered the broadside bombardment with a front-page sliding-scale comparison of baking powders. Showing absolutely pure Royal at the apex of worthiness, a long list of government chemist names followed to validate the results.

In addition to paid advertisements, Royal provided scientific-looking articles and studies to newspapers nationwide. In 1885, the *Advocate-Tribune* published a factual-looking piece of news glorifying Royal's latest innovation. Through an unexplained process, they now produced 100% pure cream of tartar, which solved the problem of impurities just by saying so.

A year later, the *Indianola-Herald* printed a five-paragraph newsworthy-looking article entitled "What Baking Powder Shall We Use?" This was Royal's counterpunch to the less expensive alum-based products now crowding the market. Claiming the Department of Agriculture's chief chemist found alum injurious, Royal's product was purest in quality and highest in strength without deleterious (toxic, harmful, lethal) substances.

In July 1888, the *Advocate-Tribune* published "A Question of Health–What Baking Powder Shall We Use?" In an unrelenting battle against competitors, Royal claimed their brand as chemically pure without the harmful effects of indigestion, dyspepsia, and evils associated with lime and alum.

The following year, Calumet in Chicago entered the battle with their alum and dried egg-white formula. They claimed Royal's product produced harmful Rochelle salts in the baking.

In 1892, the *Advocate-Tribune* published an article entitled "Alum & Ammonia In Our Bread." Claiming alum was a substitute for (more expensive) cream of tartar, a tug to motherhood heartstrings followed: "To young children, growing girls, persons of weak frame, alum bread eaten morning, noon, and evening is the most harmful." The article continued with the results of a *Scientific American* magazine analysis of the most prominent baking powders and whether they contained ammonia or alum.

In 1896, Calumet's advertisements called itself "The Standard" and acknowledged the anxiousness housewives were experiencing regarding the health of their families. In a separate article described as both solid reading material and an advertisement, Calumet disclosed promotional practices existed, but so did the concealed and harmful effects of Rochelle salts. The article ended with a push in the desired direction: "Food prepared with Calumet baking powder was entirely free from alum, Rochelle salts, alum, lime, and ammonia, or any injurious substance."

The baking powder war continued into a new century, declining only after economic advantages dissolved and new federal laws brought consequences and penalties to **Trickery And Deception** in advertising.

COLOSSAL
CLASH OF TITANS

Prohibition in Iowa wasn't working lamented the *Advocate-Tribune* in May 1887. It merely diverted the sale of intoxicants to drugstores the front-page article declared, while teaching men to be lawbreakers and leading them to all kinds of **Trickery And Deception**.

While prohibition remained intact, drugstores could legitimately sell booze for mechanical, medicinal, culinary, and sacramental purposes. Albert R Cocke, local pharmacist and dabbling meteorologist, was one such proprietor. Advertising himself as a "Druggist & Manufacturing Chemist selling Pure Wine & Spirits for Lawful Purposes," Cocke became linked to a high-profile casualty at an important time.

Dr George Bonney, local physician and surgeon, had a far-reaching practice after serving Warren County for eighteen years. Priding himself on drinking as he pleased with the ability to walk away as desired, Bonney's willpower and control succumbed to whisky's enticements. After ruining his career and home life, the good doctor became a wandering outcast.

In May 1882, Mrs Bonney took pharmacist Cocke to court for selling whisky to her husband and thereby causing his addiction and incapacitation. Represented by local real estate attorney Lewis Todhunter, retired Judge Hugh Maxwell joined the Bonney legal team.

Todhunter and Judge Maxwell were already well-known as fierce and unwavering superheroes of temperance. Bringing their message to pulpits throughout Iowa, the power of their prohibition messaging reduced anyone thinking otherwise to withering lumps of scorched flesh. Mrs Bonney likely paid little for their services.

Albert Cocke found representation in the highly respected firm of Henderson & Berry. John Hancock Henderson, son of Indianola's founding father Paris P, was born and reared in the wilderness of Warren County. William H Berry arrived to this county as a young man and graduated from Simpson Centenary College. He studied law under Judge Maxwell and later served as a State Senator to Iowa's General Assembly.

These opposing teams of colossal combatants sealed the deal for a massive lawyering-up in the case of Bonney vs Cocke. This was a real clash between titans over temperance and it happened at an important time. The following month, Iowa voters (men) would decide for or against amending our state constitution to prohibit the sale and trafficking of liquor.

The May 1882 trial of Bonney vs Cocke lasted three days before the jury awarded widow Mary $886 ($26,500 today) plus court costs. Upon appeal to Iowa's Supreme Court, the award was whittled down to withholding $115.50 against future judgements.

The June vote amending Iowa's Constitution passed but prohibition didn't last. A year later, Iowa's Supreme Court invalidated the constitutional change on a technicality, which greatly appeased Davenport's powerful and influential liquor distributors. Maxwell and Todhunter returned to advocating from the pulpit and pharmacist Cocke continued selling what was allowed.

After a good run with Dr Bozanko's cough syrup, Cocke began experimenting and manufacturing his own concoctions. He developed an adhesive and then a hair dye that did well in St Louis and Chicago. All the while he kept reporting meteorological observations to the United States Signal Services. Albert Cocke believed in the emerging science of **Foretelling The Weather** because it would someday save lives.

A STORY
OF STAYING POWER

Foretelling The Weather before the 1900s relied on mathematical calculations from respected men known as weather prophets. The most celebrated of these forecasters was Reverend Irl Hicks of St Louis.

Basing his calculations on the rotation and pathways of planets circling the sun, Hicks believed our surrounding celestial bodies, which included the disputed planet of Vulcan, created the weather. Tracking their comings and goings, the good reverend predicted perturbing influences, antagonizing storms, and all manner of weather for the upcoming year.

This well-respected weather prophet owned his own publishing company called Word & Works. Besides a weekly paper with the same name, he published a yearly weather almanac starting in1894 and continuing until his death in 1916. Early editions included his personal adage: "Prove all things, hold fast to that which is good."

Reverend Hicks believed in the consistent laws of nature, which applied to the universe. He also understood the manipulations and exploitations mankind inflicted upon our humble "Earthship" and the corresponding strains, influences, and full-blown disturbances they produced. By observing, recording, and calculating, he could arrive at reasonable conclusions and predictions. Everything in the cosmos followed the same laws. There was no such thing as devilish chaos if you studied and observed.

The emerging United States Weather Bureau, which didn't begin making weekly weather forecasts until 1908, found the work of Irl Hicks and other weather prophets scientifically bogus. Unseating the prophets as fake weather guessers of little intelligence, the bureau's meteorological experts gradually took their place.

Feeling the seasonal change, Reverend Hicks cashed-in on his star quality weather personality and hit the Chautauqua circuit as a guest speaker and lecturer.

In August 1909, Indianola's Chautauqua included Irl Hicks (Prophet), William Jennings Bryan (Lecturer), Alonzo Zwickey (Chalk-Talker or Cartoonist), and Carry A Nation of hatchet fame, along with forty local and nationally recognized speakers, singers, musicians, humorists, preachers, and entertainers.

Performing under a 50x120-foot canvas tent between the college and The Square, Chautauqua provided a wonderous time for people to gather, listen, learn, and be entertained. Carry A Nation, with a history of thirty arrests for thrashing saloons, garnered the largest audience for her lecture against drinking and smoking.

Clint Price, editor of the *Advocate-Tribune*, purposely didn't attend her diatribe but wrote, "She raw-hided President Taft, lambasted William Jennings Bryan, scores of preachers, and slandered the Masons...her lecture full of vituperations, vilifications and villainous accusations."

Those enjoying Mother Nation's virulent and violent messaging purchased souvenir pewter hatchets for their lapels. Others bought her book, "either through idle curiosity or a morbid desire to spend their money," concluded Clint Price.

Hatchet Granny accumulated great wealth with her raucous name-calling rants. Two years after Indianola's Chautauqua, she collapsed and was taken to a Leavenworth, Kansas, sanitarium, where she died.

Like most things lacking value and worth, Carry A Nation's **Over-The-Top** behavior didn't have the staying power for a steadfast legacy. She's been rightly relegated to dismissive obscurity.

GOING OVER THE TOP

During World War 1, the phrase **"Over The Top"** became irrevocably connected to describing Allied soldiers spilling from the trenches and racing headlong toward the enemy. It was also the title of a book penned by Arthur Guy Empey, an American fighting in the British Army. Advertised in Warren County's 1917 Christmas holiday newspapers, the author is pictured crouched and ready to advance with his bayonet-tipped rifle in hand.

The book held great meaning to folks back home when Indianola recruits Russell Marshall, Arch Simpson, and Edd Yates were somewhere in France. The *Indianola-Herald* had already chronicled the grim business of their Fort Dodge training before they went "over the top" for the great adventure in the trenches.

Shooting and bayonet training (always go for the throat) followed marching and drilling, which went before grenade throwing (feet apart, arms stiff) and gas demonstrations. After an unmasked taste, recruits received a full dose of chlorine or mustard gas to alleviate the initial fears of facing this terrifying enemy under wartime conditions.

Warren County's Russell Marshall was twenty years old when he enlisted, compared to Arch Simpson, who was married with thirty-two years. Edmund Yates was older and more experienced after serving in the Spanish American War and Mexican Border Campaign. All three were assigned to Company A of the 168th Infantry.

The *Indianola-Herald* and *Advocate-Tribune* regularly published letters from our boys in the trenches, and going "over the top" was never mentioned or described. However, the phrase caught fire back home as a rallying cry for exceeding Liberty Bond campaign goals and food conservation efforts. It was everyone's duty to support our boys and bring victory home.

In late May 1918, a year after enlisting, Marshall, Simpson, and Yates understood life in the trenches, bayonet battles, and gas attacks. Before the month ended, Private Russell Marshall died in hand-to-hand combat with Edd Yates and Arch Simpson seriously wounded in the same battle.

Simpson returned to his company by July with Yates needing additional time due to receiving more gas than expected. When Armistice Day arrived on the 11th month, 11th day, and 11th hour in 1918, Arch Simpson shipped home to his wife in Indianola and began selling insurance. Edd Yates lagged behind.

After acquiring tuberculosis because of poisoned water or from his already impaired health, Yates spent time in a Denver army hospital before being invalided home to Indianola.

He lived quietly until one fine day in May 1920. At nine o'clock on the courthouse lawn, Corporal Yates gave away two hundred paper kites he made during the winter. The *Advocate-Tribune* reported, "In five minutes The Square was dotted everywhere with all colors of kites being hurried homeward by their new owners."

Edd Yates died that November and lies buried at the Indianola cemetery, but his service nor his capacity for giving wasn't forgotten. The generosity of others paid for a modest headstone as well as a massive ruby red granite monument engraved with his name and service record. Remembering this **Noble Life,** we are reminded everyone has gifts to share.

REMEMBERING
A NOBLE LIFE

George Washington Carver is the very definition of a **Noble Life** and Iowa has designated February 1st of every year as a time to remember and celebrate this remarkable man. Born into slavery and experiencing repeated hardships, wrongness, and setbacks, GW Carver remained an idealist, integrating faith, education, and intellect to improve the lives of others.

His style of thinking was different and didn't follow normal pathways. Blowing past his contemporaries, Carver cultivated the idea of finding value in nuisance plants and those taken for granted, or perceived as less important. He believed a weed was only a plant out of place—like okra in a cornfield.

Honoring all living things and our natural surroundings, Carver was an early convert to reusing, recycling, and sustainability. This slightly built stooped man with a high falsetto voice was immeasurably charismatic and incredibly influential, with fresh ideas about crop rotation and safeguarding finite resources.

During a time when science and religion occupied different ends of a very long measuring stick, Carver's beliefs hinged on combining divine inspiration with scientific experimentation. He saw them as completely compatible, with inspiration never at variance with information. He believed science was about seeking the truth and the closer we came to Nature and its teachings the closer we came to the divine Creator.

While George Carver graduated from Iowa State University, his first college experience was at Indianola's Simpson College. Arriving from Winterset in 1890 to study art, after paying his matriculation fees he had only pennies and needed to find a place to live and start a business.

Seeing something special in this young man, art professor Etta May Budd introduced George Carver to Sophie and William Liston, owners of the Palace Book Store on the north side of The Square. While the Listons might have suggested the abandoned shack for his living quarters and business, they definitely helped Carver establish a line of credit to get his laundry business started.

Despite working, attending class, and studying at the same time, George Carver developed friendships among students, townsfolk, and merchants. Writing friends in Winterset, he shared the following: "The people are very kind to me here and the students are wonderfully good. They took it into their heads I was working too hard and had not enough home comforts so they clubbed together and bought me a whole set of furniture—chairs, table, bed and such things I needed."

Years later when Dr John Gross (past Simpson College president) visited Dr Carver at Tuskegee University, the scientist told him, "Everything here is the result of a vision I had while attending Simpson College."

"Just what was that vision?" asked Gross.

"At Simpson College," replied Carver, "the kind of people there made me believe I was a human being."

Improving the lives of poor farmers in "the lowlands of sorrow" became this gentle man's calling. Having February 1st **Set Aside** as George Washington Carver Day gives us time to remember him and his lessons.

RECOGNIZING THE RISE OF FLOUR POWER

Housewives had to **Set Aside** preferences in May 1903 after a fire, plainly seen from Carlisle, completely destroyed the Indianola Novelty Roller Mill. No longer would families savor bread, cakes, and biscuits from locally milled Our Pride, Snow Flake, or Golden Harvest flour with a fifty-pound sack costing less than a dollar.

While the mill on the corner of North 1st and East Boston experienced several renovations and fires during its lifetime, this final conflagration ended an era of local flour milling. It also coincided with Iowa's downward trajectory as a heavyweight wheat producer.

Like new ingredients in an old recipe, the consistency of our local marketplace was changing. The flours from massive mills in neighboring states were now populating grocery store shelves. There was Ben-Hur, Pillsbury's Best, and Sleepy-Eye flours from Minnesota and Zephyr from Lawrence, Kansas, with locally produced Valley Lilly from Milo Mills still clinging to some store shelves.

As Indianola housewives dipped their measuring cups into flour sacks to knead, coax, and carefully watch the rising of their daily bread, a dusting of better times approached. In 1911, brothers Peter and Charley Zondervan started a bakery business on the west side of The Square.

A decade later and despite a small fire, the Zondervans' bakery was flourishing. Two loaves of Indian-Ola-Maid white bread baked daily and wrapped in waxed paper cost a whopping twenty-five cents, with cakes, cookies, and buns also available. As the success of this family business continued to rise, so did bread baking outside the home. Women had better things to do.

In September 1932, the *Indianola-Tribune* reported Wonder Bread would supply all the bread for a state-wide Democratic barbeque and rally in Indianola. This nationwide brand, with its familiar Slo-Baked logo, came already sliced and guaranteed not to quickly dry.

Fortunately, the Zondervans could address this cutting-edge innovation. A few years prior, Otto Frederick Todwedder of Davenport invented and patented a machine capable of making uniform bread slices while keeping the loaf together for packaging.

On June 1st 1933, the *Indianola-Record* reported Zondervans' bread could now be sliced by machinery with sharp knives without pressing and the new slices actually tasted better.

The idea of perfect toast in the morning and uniform sandwich slices in the afternoon forever changed the bakery business and our eating habits. It created the "Best Thing Since Sliced Bread" expression we continue using for anything new and amazing.

Despite these best efforts, Zondervans' Bakery followed the same recipe as the local flour milling business. Closing their bakery in 1939 after twenty-eight years, bread-bearing trucks traipsing down from Des Moines were squeezing the market, which is never good for bread.

The **Ebb And Flow** of this story isn't sad if we recognize and appreciate the ongoing evolution of flour power. Today, the white variety no longer rules as we savor a diversity of grains in the making and baking of our daily bread.

STUMBLING ON HOMETOWN HISTORY PART 1

A hundred years ago, the **Ebb And Flow** of the times produced a Ku Klux Klan revival. Claiming not to be an enemy of the Negro but desiring white supremacy, Klan members believed they'd been disenfranchised by Catholics and Jews in government, and they also considered immigrants a dangerous unhealthy influence. They would reckon these wrongs and restore America to great again.

Dr NC Carpenter, pastor of the Capital Hill Christian Church in Des Moines, became a recognized Klan spokesperson in Warren County. Sermonizing the invisible empire had every right to organize and parade in hooded white garments, he proclaimed that the Klan's nationwide membership surpassed three million native-born white Protestant Americans.

In June 1923, secret and secluded Klan initiation ceremonies took place in Lacona, New Virginia, and Indianola, which included burning fiery crosses in the eerie time around midnight. The *Lacona Ledger* and *Indianola-Record* reported these events while editorializing, "the restless and discontented should settle down, stay home a little more, attend church more regularly, and be more neighborly."

In September that year, Dr Thomas Roberts, recently excised as the Iowa American Legion chaplain for his "Klannishness," addressed a multitude on the Warren County courthouse lawn. Don Berry, editor of the *Indianola-Record*, remarked, "Hundreds of people accepted the platitudes and threadbare Americanism at face value and took no trouble to look between the sentences."

Editor Berry later received a Klan backlash for sharing a strategy Dr Roberts mentioned during his speech. "The purpose of the Klan," he told the audience, "Was to concentrate into a potential force the strength of those Protestants who are not affiliated with any church organization."

In other words, the hooded order wanted to gather and pull together the strength and power of fear-filled individuals in order to focus their fear and hate on targeted people.

Dr Carpenter from Des Moines returned to Indianola in May 1924 professing every classroom needed to add Americanism and daily Bible reading to their curriculum. "Purity, sanctity, dignity and simplicity of the American home, must be upheld," he declared. He asked the aroused crowd if every Protestant should join the Klan and if they found honor in membership. Both statements received a chorus of supportive shouts and cheers.

Leveraging patriotism, God, and country, the Klan sponsored a grand parade that year. With hooded men on white horses leading a sixty-piece band around The Square, they were followed by beautiful floats and five hundred white-robed marching members. The *Indianola-Record* reported their nighttime fireworks display was the most gorgeous ever seen in Warren County.

The following year, the Klan added a towering burning cross to their repertoire. Long after midnight, a steady stream of slow-moving cars filled the Jefferson Highway bound for home.

Don Berry wrote in the early days of this resurgence, "The Klan is merely a dramatic example of the general spirit of intolerance—a spirit which has come before and may come again."

Reflecting on a fringe group's rebellion at our nation's capital and Iowa's continued push towards book banning, public school defunding, women and gender disregarding initiatives—**Pshaw.** Here we are again.

STUMBLING ON
HOMETOWN HISTORY
PART 2

Researching Warren County newspapers and stumbling across an explosion of Ku Klux Klan activity during the 1920s brought questions, shock, and disappointment. However, this surge wasn't unique to Warren County; it happened throughout Iowa and the Midwest.

Talking with others, a friend mentioned having a Klan robe in the eaves of her family home. Knowing a Ku Klux Klan member's robe constitutes their most recognizable symbol, I asked to take a picture. She agreed as long as I didn't use her real name. We arranged to meet a week later at the Warren County Historical Society & Museum.

The robe arrived in a large cardboard Montgomery Ward box tied with a thin strip of cotton cloth. Inside lay a neatly folded ivory-colored muslin-like garment. It was intact, somewhat discolored, and in very good shape. The one-size-fits-all design with matching buttons down the front was belted by a tasseled cord. The large attached hood left the face uncovered. A brilliant red and black embroidered patch over the heart held a drop of blood inside a black diamond at the center of a stylized cross.

We put the robe on a dressmaker's mannequin for viewing and then quickly returned it to the box before the museum opened.

"I've known for most of my life it was up there, under the eaves, where no one knew about it," Sue explained. "I was young when I first saw it. Don't know who it belonged to, both sides of my family were (Warren County) early settlers."

"It's not acceptable to talk about," she continued. "Whoever in my family owned it might be rolling over in their grave. I have a mixed family, and while we have different wrapping paper on the outside, we are the same family inside."

Given that Warren County newspapers began reporting Klan events in 1923, we surmised the robe was likely from that time.

"It's nothing to be proud of, but it's history," Sue surmised. "How appropriate would it be to throw that baby on a fire?" she continued, reflecting on the robe. "Part of my head says how can I destroy history? The other part says, what am I going to do with it?"

Leo Landis, Curator of Museum and Historic Sites for the Iowa State Historical Society, confirmed Iowa experienced a great depth of Klan activism in the 1920s. He also acknowledged that it was a shocking period of Iowa history to stumble upon. In terms of what to do with the robe, Landis commented, "They are not unusual in family and museum collections due to the Klan's prevalence in Iowa. We have two, and I know of several others at county historical museums."

Despite this acknowledgment, it didn't solve Sue's problem. "I have five generations of things in my house," she explained. "That's how it ended up in my house. It never left. Maybe I'll leave it and someone might find it someday. I just don't want them to think it was mine."

Pshaw!

LAMENTING
NEW TECHNOLOGY

Pshaw, Clint Price, owner of the *Advocate-Tribune*, lamented in his December 16th 1909 "Whispers Whispered" front page column. The invention of the telephone made it impossible to hide a person's whereabouts. After repeated calls and failures to answer, husbands could no longer claim they were at the office and wives couldn't pretend to be at home.

Almost thirty years prior to Price's observation, linking homes and businesses together via a telephone exchange remained an elusive Indianola aspiration. The *Advocate-Tribune* began promoting the idea in 1882 after reporting advancements in nearby towns: Creston's exchange had one hundred subscribers, Osceola published a telephoned story, and 105 miles between Sterling, Illinois and Muscatine, Iowa were now linked by poles and wires with a central operator.

The establishment of an Indianola phone system sputtered and died in May 1882 when only nineteen subscribers committed. However, the *Advocate-Tribune* wasn't deterred and kept pushing. Reporting in October that all neighboring county seats possessed a telephone system might have been the tipping point.

The following month, the Indianola Telephone Exchange was born with a central office inside Thomas Crosthwait's harness shop on The Square's east side. Linking Indianola, Summerset, and Carlisle, there was also a line through Des Moines providing connectivity to Winterset. With service payable quarterly and in advance, businesses could join for fifty dollars per year and residences at a more affordable thirty dollars.

The *Indianola-Herald* provided pointers on proper etiquette in a two-column piece entitled "Telephone Peculiarities." With emphasis on not shouting into the instrument, persons were advised to speak normally and deliberately, while articulating clearly, and to employ good plain English.

A year later, Indianola's telephone service included fifty-two instruments and was described as "good." A delighted city council passed an ordinance allowing the exchange to use any street or alley they desired for poles, wires, and fixtures.

The telephone quickly moved from convenience to necessity, with persistent excitement for its reported usefulness in the newspapers:

- "We learned by Telephone that a valuable brown mare weighing 1050 lbs and having a large white spot on (its) hip was stolen from Mr. Falwell, near Patterson, last night. No clues as yet."

- "Johnson, Olive & Olive (north side of Square) have just put in a telephone and will promptly attend to all calls of customers over the wire."

- "The Drake University nine who were to play our college nine last Friday sent a telephone message to the effect they would not come."

Over two thousand telephones connected Warren County subscribers (population nearly 20,000) when Clint Price published his 1909 lamentation. All of them tethered to local exchanges with a bevy of central operators connecting the parties.

Cherished for their service, these dedicated working women held vast reservoirs of information. Proud of their service, mentioned years later in their obituaries, they knew everything about everybody with handy access to baseball scores, election results, accidents, fires, deaths, and births.

This made **Back When** a more pleasurable experience as compared to phone trees and call centers today.

TRUTH AND OPINION
IN REPORTING

Back When local correspondents sent reports on the comings and goings in their communities to Indianola newspapers, they sometimes needed to be reminded not to predict the weather and refrain from prophesizing weddings. Timely submissions were encouraged, as well as good composition, penmanship, and truthfulness.

Reporting on the sick and improved in March 1885, Ackworth's local correspondent for the *Advocate-Tribune* also reported Steven Wilson received a $2.50 fine for spitting on the library floor. This same correspondent also seemed fixated on the whereabouts of Mr Elwood Hiatt. The man's location was reported every week starting in early 1885, and then the notifications stopped mid-year. It didn't take long for Palmyra's correspondent to request an update, which was dutifully delivered. Mr Hiatt had returned home to rest and was now harvesting.

In February 1886, Bevington's local correspondent for the *Advocate-Tribune* reported that "Wm Hugghart, who is deformed in his lower extremities, is under the care of Dr Blond of New York." The following week, a letter to the editor from Mr Hugghart informed readers his reported physical curiosity was a "pine blank lie." Directly following, editor William Schooley cautioned local correspondents to confine themselves to the domain of truth.

That same month, a firestorm ignited between Lacona correspondents from both of Indianola's newspapers. The first volley from the *Advocate-Tribune* disputed Brother Willey's historical accuracy during a Methodist revival meeting. Cyrus likely didn't use cannon fire during the siege of Babylon. Additionally, the good reverend was mistaken when he proclaimed a nonbeliever's taste in literature didn't rise above a dime novel. Editor Schooley agreed with the historical error but didn't respond to the reading and comprehension levels of heathens.

The *Indianola-Herald's* Lacona correspondent characterized the *Advocate's* correspondent as "venting a little spleen." Furthermore, "intelligent readers should treat these kinds of commentaries with the contempt they deserve." This flaming missive was signed "Guest."

At the end of February, a letter published in the *Herald* from the *Advocate's* correspondent asked Guest to reveal themselves rather than strike like an assassin. Signing her letter, "Respectfully yours, Mrs Josie Morley," this battle was just getting started.

In mid-March, the *Herald's* Lacona correspondent reported the roads were muddy due to snow melt, the schools were running nicely, Reverend Willey began another lengthy effort in Liberty Center, and Guest's opinion belonged to someone else. However, signing the column "Dido" left considerable doubt about which side this correspondent was taking.

On April 1st, Mrs Morley reported for the *Advocate* that Andy Kesler lost a horse, George Clever and Nels Jacobs shipped two carloads of hogs, and she would never war against a foe unworthy of her steel. Likening personal sneers to water rolling off a duck's back, it was her God-given right to think for herself.

At one time or another, these local correspondents sandwiched an opinion or unflattering comment in their reporting. They also asked questions we might ponder today. **What's The Trouble** with pigs up on Otter Creek? We will never know.

FINDING UNEXPECTED GREATNESS

What's The Trouble with all able-bodied males in Indianola providing two days of hard labor to maintain our streets, alleys, and sidewalks? While this requirement for men (only) between the ages of eighteen and forty-five years had been in place for some time, it became City Ordinance #11 in 1882 and was identified as a poll tax.

Poll taxes had been around since colonial times and were originally unrelated to voting. They constituted a per person or per head form of taxation where everyone was treated the same, regardless of income or resources.

Indianola's poll tax for conscripted labor was under the supervision of the street commissioner, who could summon a much-needed workforce anytime from April through August. Those failing to appear or provide a suitable substitute were fined three dollars per day. Those deemed physically unable were excused with their names published in the newspaper.

Since the Indianola Street Commissioner didn't have a budget or equipment, every poll tax participant brought their own tools, along with horses and wagons, to complete their two ten-hour work days. In addition to directing a hodgepodge of workers, the commissioner tracked all no-shows, substitutes, and delinquencies. Besides being a cumbersome administrative process, participant responsibility was likely inconsistent and a nuisance.

Near the end of 1884, 221 able-bodied Indianola males responded to the poll tax calling and an early pioneer named Andy Park was named street commissioner. While they didn't know it at the time, Indianola's city council made a near perfect selection.

Andy Park had already earned his status as an old landmark of Indianola. Arriving in Warren County in 1852 with a wife and several children in the company of four other families, they were all from Indiana. Settling inside the boundaries of White Oak Township, a wild country where nature still ruled, they survived and prospered. Their line of farmsteads became known as Hoosier Row.

Park served in several city-appointed positions before becoming street commissioner, which is where he became best known. His skills and services were highly appreciated, persistently requested, and he tried retiring several times.

Thinking he was retiring, Andy Park would thank city council members for their kindness and invite them to an oyster supper at his expense. However, his replacement never quite worked and this now elderly pioneer was soon returned to manipulating the grader, coordinating spring cleanings, and keeping streets in good working order. Attempting to retire again, there would be another oyster supper offering.

Commissioner Park finally retired in 1894 and died before a successor could be named. After his funeral, a remarkable procession followed his remains to the cemetery. It was a clear demonstration of the high esteem everyone held for this good and humble man.

Andre W Park's grave is Row 1 and Plot 1 of the Old IOOF section of the cemetery. Could this **Honored Position** have been happenstance or does it forever recognize and remember a life of good and quiet greatness?

WISDOM FROM
YESTERYEAR

The **Honored Position** of teaching has always been underpaid and overworked. "Why," the *Warren County Leader* lamented in 1871, "when so much of the nation's future greatness depends on it."

This time-honored problem continues today, but with a difference. Compulsory education in Iowa wasn't required years ago despite Warren County teachers, our learned professionals, continually advocating for it. Elected officials didn't listen until 1902, when educating all young minds was finally required by the Iowa legislature.

Arguments against mandated education included calling it a state intrusion, loss of liberty, and anti-American. Truth be known, Iowa's rural school systems didn't want to lose control. Looking into deeper darker backwaters, pulling children from the fields to attend school seemed another rationale.

In December 1890, prior to legislating compulsory education, the *Indianola-Herald* reported that Professor Delancy Michener, Indianola School Superintendent, provided an excellent talk on the subject. "It will cost no more to educate all," Michener argued while explaining, "Education is the strong pillar of government and should be strengthened by forcing the careless to educate their children."

The following year Prof Michener was relieved of his superintendent position on the 109th ballot by Indianola school board members during a meeting extending into the wee hours of early morning. At the same meeting, it took between thirty and forty ballots to continue the employment of two teachers.

The *Advocate-Tribune* surmised these drawn-out antics and misbehaviors resulted from personal differences between school board members and were unrelated to superintendent and teacher performance. After ousting the popular Professor Delancy Michener, the school board appointed a recent Simpson College graduate to the position of Indianola Schools Superintendent.

The following week, after the board increased the school calendar from eight months to nine, a petition with two hundred signatures from school patrons and friends was delivered and read aloud. The petition opposed displacing Prof Michener and requested, with sincerity and respect, his immediate reinstatement.

An oppressive silence followed until a board member spoke about recognizing the constitutional right to petition and request action. Following another awkward stillness, another board member made a motion aligning with the petition's request. The motion was seconded, and a vote taken to reinstate Prof Michener. The six-member board tied with three ayes and three nays, which meant Delancy Michener would not return to his position.

Before the year ended, an event of uncommon proportions transpired. In a fit of rage, possibly fueled by inexperience and workplace stress, the new school superintendent severely whipped an unruly student, breaking twelve switches across the lad's back, neck, and arms. After being dismissed by the school board, he was arrested for assault and battery with intent to deliver great bodily injury.

With the politically motivated demise of an experienced superintendent followed by his replacement's career-ending behavior, the *Advocate-Tribune* declared, "Our schools are now in a crisis."

Comparing yesteryear to today, it's **Crystal Clear** unfortunate pathways and outcomes can be avoided if elected officials trust their professionals and listen to the people.

FINDING A SOLID CRYSTAL CLEAR PATH

Crystal Clear and free of contaminants is how everyone wanted their ice delivered in the spring of 1900, and Will Demory delivered a pure, clean, and solid product. "Warm Weather Was Coming, It Was Time To Get Your Refrigeration Ready!" read his April advertisement in the *Indianola-Herald*.

After a customer placed an order at Osborne's Pharmacy or called the Demory household, prompt delivery naturally followed. Multiple horse-drawn wagons made daily runs throughout Indianola. Refrigeration kept food safe and sweet, and everyone knew sour milk made a bitter man.

Will Demory came to Warren County with his pioneer parents and remained a solid citizen throughout his life. Farming with his father and later for himself while supporting a family of six children, he saw the economic advantages of harvesting a readily available commodity in large quantities. Additionally, harvesting winter ice didn't impact his farming and dairy business.

His ice business continued expanding and in 1918 Will Demory built a new ice pond on the South River. Damming the water's flow and waiting for a cold spell of strong duration, he knew a steady unbroken freeze without thaws or snow created crystal clear heavy ice.

The Demory Ice Company eventually owned a large ice house three blocks north of The Square's northeast corner, opposite the Rock Island Station. Using the most modern equipment, service and deliveries were guaranteed year-round.

However, ice refrigeration couldn't compete with electric refrigeration. In late 1927, the Empress Theatre advertised a free demonstration of the Frigidaire,

General Motors' electric refrigerator. In the same issue, Indianola's city council said they would lower electric rates.

The first reported installation of a Frigidaire in Warren County might have been the previous year in William Beardsley's New Virginia pharmacy. His eight-compartment unit, installed by experts from the Delco Light Company (General Motors subsidiary) kept a variety of ice cream flavors good and solid.

With the onset of this new technology, Demory Ice Company's advertisements slid into claiming their lower-cost refrigeration method remained safe and silent while protecting food and flavors. However, the glamour and enticement of electric refrigeration was attracting a multitude of converts. Will Demory must have recognized the frosted walls of his iceboxes melting into obscurity.

In the summer of 1927, Beardsley's pharmacy advertised peanut brittle as their weekend ice cream special. In addition to dispensing medications and servicing a busy soda fountain, store merchandise included wallpaper to freshen drab surfaces, the latest in Parker pens, Dr Hess' Horse Tonic and Poultry Panacea, and film supplies to "Keep a KODAK record of the children."

Entering politics while running a bustling business, Republican Bill Beardsley served in the Iowa Senate and was re-elected. Later, while filling a seat in the House, he pursued running against Iowa's two-term incumbent Republican governor.

Given little hope of winning but having the support of organized labor and educators, a massive Democratic crossover swept this small-town New Virginia pharmacist into the governor's mansion.

Ignoring Party Leaders, Iowa hearts followed their core values and Governor-elect Beardsley celebrated by serving Cokes and coffee from behind the counter of his soda fountain.

RISE TO SHINE TO THINK FOR YOURSELF

Ignoring Party Leaders and taking an independent position was Warren Blade's advice in a letter to the editor published by the *Weekly Indianola-Visitor* on December 16th 1858. Like most opinions penned at the time, the name was a pseudonym. Despite the anonymity, Editor James H Knox encouraged the free-thinking individual to keep writing.

Knox began publishing the *Visitor* in April 1857 after acquiring the printing equipment from the defunct *Indianola Republican*. While James Knox believed in fair dealings, truthfulness, and not heaping abuse and maliciousness on a single party or candidate, he knew following an independent path of thinking would catch considerable heat.

Regardless of the consequences and about the same time as Warren Blade's letter, the *Visitor* firmly declared itself as an independent publication. Announcing the stance included a guiding principle on the front page: "Equal and Exact Justice to All—Special Favors to None."

In early 1860, James Knox headed to Pikes Peak gold rush and left his newspaper in capable and trusted hands. Returning five months later to accusations the *Visitor* was running on Democratic money, Editor Knox responded with a scathing rebuttal.

After disclosing the totality of the newspaper's financial affairs, Knox emphasized no special payments were made to Democratic candidates and persons from both parties as well as undeclared voters supported his publication. Declaring the *Visitor* had been unfairly judged, Knox further emphasized those saying otherwise had burnt themselves and "you can now SIT ON THE BLISTERS."

However, with the 1860 election of Republican Abraham Lincoln as president quickly followed by the firing upon Fort Sumter, maintaining an independent position proved impossible. Knox hoisted the Republican flag and followed his beliefs by serving as Captain of Iowa's 34th Infantry Company D in the Great American Army (GAR).

After serving, Knox returned to Indianola as postmaster and co-owner of the *Weekly-Herald*. Remaining unafraid and politically motivated, years later he was described as a "pungent paragraphist...master of invective (criticism) and satire...generally found at the head of the fraction that carried the day."

Owing to his penetrating literary abilities, Knox's opinions didn't follow Iowa's smooth and rolling landscape. His thoughts issued forth with thunderous eruptions and plunging downpours while delivering blistering notions and provocative viewpoints.

In 1878, Indianola's other Republican newspaper, the *Warren Record*, unleashed a column entirely devoted to the well-known editor. Labeling Knox a "Political Skunk," the paper described him as a man of obnoxious stench, devoid of conscience, worshiping only himself, and fighting anyone he couldn't control.

In 1880, James Knox left the newspaper business and Indianola. Moving with his wife to forty acres west of Des Moines, they owned a "modern home" with water pipes, gas lighting, and fixtures readily convertible to electricity. Their surrounding acres of orchards, vineyards, and impeccably maintained barns created a working farm we can only dream about.

No longer wielding a sword of piercing political prose, some believed Knox left Indianola badly demoralized, hard, and stern. However, succumbing to a seductive bucolic life while remaining well-read and politically influential sounds like achieving a **Loftier Aspiration**. Perhaps it was something others simply couldn't accept.

DESPITE ALL ODDS, A GREAT SPIRIT SURVIVES

Arthur Wherry Richards, a man of **Loftier Ambitions**, came to Indianola in 1854 at twenty-three years of age. Describing this place as a vast prairie with few settlers, he wrote, "The town's two-story courthouse, church and school built by people low in numbers showed good sense, forethought, and energy. It was a small beginning in the right direction."

AW Richards married and fathered ten children, with the greater half arriving before the 1861 call to join the Great American Army (GAR) in the War of the Rebellion.

Contracting malaria, as did many in Company G of the 3rd Iowa Infantry, he continued soldiering with head buzzing, joints stiffening, and bullets flying. Fever and exhaustion accompanied his every move over days of heat and torrential rains in sultry conditions.

Taking a leap from a train into a nearby ditch, Arthur later surmised his "starchy condition" caused a lower back injury leading to his discharge in June 1862. Returning home, pain soon encompassed his entire spinal cord, which eventually bent inward, issuing forth pus and gore over the course of a decade. At that point, Arthur Wherry Richards lost total use of his legs but did his best to remain "pleasant, cheerful, and keep in the sunlight."

Opening a real estate office for properties to rent, sell, and buy, he also sold New Home sewing machines and magnetic goods. When military pensions became available, AW Richards prepared applications for many widows and families. In 1884, the *Advocate-Tribune* reported, "Miss Fanny Chapman of this place received a back pension of $1896 and eight dollars a month for life."

Using these funds to modify the family home on south Howard, the Richards residence became a landmark embodying eccentric architectural detail.

Arthur W Richards was also an inventor with patented designs, one of his first being a perambulating cot or invalid chair. Pushed daily to his "Intelligence Office," he conducted business and received guests to "disfuse intelligence." He also patented a two-row corn harvester and husk shredder with nine-foot wheels riding above the corn. His prototype tipped the Novelty Mill's scale at 7,600 pounds and was the only one ever built.

Periodically writing newspaper opinions and articles like "Short Speeches by Old Settlers," he published a memoir with poetry and reflections in September 1892. His 355-page tome, *Progress of Life and Thought*, remains in print, although not at the original $2.50 price. His preface poem sheds light on the man:

> "Let us gather up the sunbeams
> Lying all around our path;
> Let us keep the wheat and roses
> Casting out the thorns and chaff
> Let us find our sweetest comforts
> In the blessings of to-day
> With a patient hand removing
> All the briars from the way."

Despite great physical suffering, AW kept a smiling face and ran for office in the Iowa legislature. Believing honest people could settle their differences in all but criminal cases, it's likely he didn't garner campaign support from Indianola attorneys. He believed in tax equalization and cheap schoolbooks while opposing rings, cliques, trusts, and boot-leg saloons. He lost the election and tried again, but graciously withdrew upon declaring he was seeking every possible way to be useful and serve the public.

This well-known early pioneer **Burned Bright** until January 2nd 1915. At eighty-two years of age Arthur Wherry Richards passed away at home surrounded by his blessed wife and nine children.

THEN AND NOW
@ YEAR'S END

According to the owners of the *Indianola-Herald* and *Advocate-Tribune*, who found little agreement on anything, 1890 **Burned Bright** after the previous year when many left Warren County.

After an unfavorable harvest, business decline, and dissatisfaction with the handling of public affairs, glib-tongued speculators convinced many in the county to join the Oklahoma Land Rush. "It seemed almost a stampede," the *Advocate-Tribune* surmised.

The rush for two million acres of Oklahoma land on April 22nd 1889 left everyone back in Iowa listless and likely envious. Fighting melancholy, Indianola's city council discussed making an improvement. There were meetings, courthouse speeches, and debates on street corners about a waterworks, library, or city administration building. In March 1890, the people voted to build an electric light plant.

Without a hitch, wiggle, or bobble, a brick structure with a tall smokestack for the modern Edison System materialized on the same ground where Indianola Municipal Utility (IMU) sits today. All summer long, a team of men erected pine poles busily and noisily around The Square and down side streets, which were laced with wire for the coursing and flowing of the upcoming wonderment.

Taking this quantum leap, a divided people joined together in an explosion of confidence and community spirit. Among them were the Anderson brothers, owners of the *Indianola-Herald*. They moved their office into better quarters on The Square, invested in electric lights, and bought a new steam engine for their press.

The twenty-year-old courthouse received a fresh coat of paint and a new steam heating system at great expense ($5,000). The jail, part of the sheriff's house and not attached to the courthouse, remained little-used due to strict enforcement of prohibition laws.

Simpson College's new Ladies Hall (Mary Berry) wasn't available until winter term but the newly completed Science Hall (Wallace) held classes during the 1890 fall term. After climbing stairs to the high-ceilinged skylighted third floor, George Washington Carver attended art classes there. He was likely present when the switch was thrown to electrify The Square in mid-September.

With twenty miles of good sidewalks, Indianola was described as a community of church-goers proud of their 2,254-volume public library with the "very best kind of reading materials." Trusting their professionals, librarian Hannah Babb was declared the most competent person in the county on the subject of books.

In a show of county-wide community pride, rural residents reported, "Indianola was coming out all right." Despite another year of drought and below average crops, county farmers prospered sending 104,000 hogs and 15,000 head of cattle to market along with Silas Keeney's estimate of 1,400 horses. Adding poultry, butter, eggs, oats, potatoes, and old corn, 1890 farm export estimates swelled to a whopping two million dollars.

Yet despite electricity's exuberant expansion accompanied by spreading abundance and enterprising in all directions, Indianola and Warren County remained steadfast. Resisting a path of wild excitement, rampant speculation, and impetuous governing, this place remained quietly energetic. **Then And Now**, a good place to call home.

FINDING MIDDLE GROUND AND ROAD FORWARD

Then And Now, the steady advance of modern influences on young minds hasn't diminished the worry and concern it brings to more aged intellects. Indianola's introduction to automobiles and motion pictures over a hundred years ago is a shining example of this persistent generational divide.

In 1905, Chris Schreiber, a skilled blacksmith, was first to sell and repair automobiles in Indianola. Two years later, he established the first moving picture theatre on The Square's north side. The following year, Vatier Loring opened the Crystal Theatre on the west side before opening his own automobile garage. Loring sold the five-passenger Maxwell and Overland touring cars while Schreiber sold the Des Moines-built Mason series.

In 1908, the Crystal Theatre's advertisements boasted "Our Song Slides Are The Best," while Schreiber's Lyric Theatre advertised silent new releases like *Wrongly Accused* or *A Wife's Devotion*, which required tag-along spoken explanations. Two years later, with a dozen automobiles circling The Square, Schreiber and Loring sold their theatre interests to focus on the automobile. The *Advocate-Tribune* declared, "The horseless carriage has come to stay."

Meanwhile, the perceived negative influence of motion pictures on young minds was rising like the tension in a high-octane thriller. In October 1911, when the Lyric re-opened after re-modeling, which included installing a fresh air ventilation system, Indianola's high school seniors attended the premiere with chaperones.

The following month, after a benefit at the Crystal Theatre for a Simpson student breaking his leg on the football field, the faculty announced a ban against theatre-going. Dredging up a long-standing but ignored policy against attending plays, students would now suffer the consequences. Writing about these times, historian Joseph Walt (*Beneath the Whispering Maples*) surmised, "Students in Indianola were increasingly disposed to test the moral resolve of their mentors."

On December 14th the *Advocate-Tribune* reported Simpson President Strickland had evidence of low scholarship due to excessive social activities. Since students weren't finding time to do their work, outdoor social functions would now be chaperoned by faculty members.

The junior class responded with a proposal urging college faculty to lift the embargo and allow "good plays." At the same time, the Crystal Theatre's showing of *Dante's Inferno* was described as a masterpiece, which the *Indianola-Herald* further noted: "In view of its educational, literary, and religious value, this is conceded to be the greatest (movie) of modern times. Admission twenty-five cents."

At the start of a new year, President Strickland secured prominent pulpit orator and alumnus Reverend Charles Blair for a week of lectures to improve the religious life of students. The following month, Simpson held its annual Founders and Benefactor Day Celebration, which meant no classes. Town and gown came together for a day of plays and musical song (dancing still prohibited) followed by a banquet and a basketball game ending with a hometown win.

Not another word crept into the newspapers about the theatre ban or junior class proposal. Attitudes were likely shifting towards **Middle Ground** because more important things needed consideration—Indianola and Warren County needed better roads for the automobile.

LOYALTY,
A MOVING TARGET

In February 1918, loyalty had no **Middle Ground**. The United States was midway through its first world war with our boys in the trenches fighting autocratic domination and foreign control. Everyone back home was scrimping on flour and sugar, saving whatever they could for the upcoming "3d Liberty Loan Campaign."

The following month, the *Indianola-Herald* reported William Buxton Sr, early settler and patron of Indianola and Simpson College, died. In addition to the front-page headline and picture, a two-paragraph commentary on page two described this early pioneer as central to the development of Warren County. Using the word "loyalty" three times in the snippet, the Buxton commentary was sandwiched between two similarly infused paragraphs touting the need for aggressive patriotism and weeding out of German sympathizers. Men must decide if they were patriots or traitors; there was no middle ground.

Mr Buxton's long obituary, also on page two, mentioned living in Warren County for sixty-five years and his importance among business circles while experiencing well-deserved prosperity. He'd given land for Indianola's first city park and donated fifty-thousand dollars ($1.8M today) to Simpson College.

This dedicated loyalist died in California after a lifetime of going the distance and returned to Indianola's IOOF Cemetery for burial. Born in Derbyshire, England, William Buxton made his way to Warren County on horseback in the winter of 1852 at twenty years of age. Buying land near Carlisle, which included a sturdy log home, he married, accumulated more land, prospered, and built a fine frame home.

Before moving to Indianola in 1893, Buxton founded Warren County Bank with his namesake son and other business leaders. At his time of death, bank advertisements suggested residents should open a saving account in readiness for the upcoming 3d Liberty Loan Campaign. Deposits would accumulate interest after sixty days.

At the time of his father's passing, Buxton-the-Younger, middle-aged and experienced in farming, business, and banking, was serving as our county's wartime food administrator. He was responsible for enforcing sugar and flour allowances. If a guideline changed and a household now held a surplus, it needed to be returned.

During this same month, the *Advocate-Tribune* reported on the first military funeral at St Marys Immaculate Church. The service was for Frank Bussanmus and Reverend Minch preached from the Gospel of Matthew about rendering to Caesar what was his and to God what was God's. Returning to modern times in his sermonizing, the good reverend likened elected and public officials to having a mantle of authority akin to the Almighty. He said it was the sacred duty of every American to render loyal obedience to our "constituted authority."

During this first world war, you were either all in or you were the enemy. There was no middle ground because this war-to-end-all-wars would make the world safe for democracy. Those elected or given legitimate power (our constituted authorities) were never openly ridiculed or threatened. It was unthinkable.

Loyalty and patriotism are different today but elections can still surprise. Recent elections demonstrated a majority will vote for what's right and decent regardless of party lines. Nothing was said, no hints given, but the unexpected coming together created a **Brilliantly Bright Moment**.

FINDING
COMMON GROUND

Brilliantly Bright Moments from our past are everywhere if enough pieces are found. Patching story fragments together could be akin to working an archeological dig without mud and dust but they don't always deliver a Hallmark-happy ending.

"Why shouldn't Warren County farmers have a stock exchange?" wrote William H Schooley, editor of the *Advocate-Tribune* in February 1885. He'd just added a "Live Stock Exchange" to his front page and for a nickel a line, farmers could advertise the sale of milch cows, Short Horn bulls, stock hogs, Norman brood mares, and mules.

Confessing he wanted the exchange to increase patronage and subscriptions, Schooley placed it on the left side of the front page. Below animal offerings were paid advertisements for attorneys, physicians, dentists, and other professionals.

Later that year, David Kyle of Xenia, Ohio visited his son Samuel, who owned four hundred acres near Ackworth. Sometime during the visit, this father and son duo took editor Schooley's idea up a notch. They organized a monthly live livestock sale with Samuel running the business and his father serving as a silent partner after returning home to Ohio.

Commencing in January of the new year and with city council permission, Indianola's first livestock sale took place on The Square. Hotels and livery stables supported the effort by offering half-price rates and downtown merchants contributed with special sales at rock-bottom prices.

Building his business on low commissions, excellent auctioneers, outstanding stock, and fair treatment, Samuel placed advertisements in both Indianola newspapers. They appeared vastly different due to printing press and typeset limitations. The simpler *Indianola-Herald* included the goal of this new endeavor: "These stock sales are for the purpose of bringing buyer and seller on common ground."

In March, the *Indianola-Herald's* pre-sale notice boasted a livestock array of four full-blooded Short Horn bulls, three stallions, twenty-four brood hogs, fifteen roadster and draft horses, twenty thoroughbred Short Horn cattle, and several parties looking for fine driving horses. All this in addition to normal business on The Square!

This brilliant idea started withering under August heat and humidity. Additionally, Samuel and his father David were taken to court by Orasmus Nelson Young, a local farmer and auctioneer. The dispute was settled when the judge awarded $538.61 ($17,600 today) plus attorney fees to Mr Orasmus Young.

At the same time, the monthly livestock sale was pushed off The Square. While continuing as scheduled, it jockeyed between the fairgrounds and a piece of open ground between Indianola's two flour mills. Undoubtedly, businesses on The Square may have tired of livestock disruptions, carnage, and clean-up.

A year later in March 1887, all four hundred acres of Samuel's land was transferred to the Kings Great Western Powder Company of Xenia, Ohio. While the gunpowder company had no use for Warren County land, they'd come to Iowa seeking payment in a legal dispute. Immediately after the ownership change, King's Great dropped their lawsuit against David and his father.

Without land and holding a partially busted business, Samuel left Warren County. He traveled to western Iowa, married and divorced, then moved to Montana, where he lived with his identical twin William.

While Indianola was never home, Samuel's ingenuity and risk-taking **Breaking New Ground** is a part of history worth discovering and piecing together.

INDIANOLA'S PIED PIPER

Early settler Joel Jacoby epitomizes **Breaking New Ground**. Arriving in 1855 as a trained cobbler, Jacoby expanded his repertoire into a more lucrative harness-making operation.

Instrumental in bringing the iron horse to Indianola in 1871, which also brought the telegraph, Joel Jacoby could see the direction of community growth and opportunity. Returning home from eastbound travels the following year, he noticed businesses in towns with manufacturing plants were lively and good while towns without that direction were missing something.

Joel Jacoby wasn't the only one feeling this way. In February 1873, Iowa's Industrial Convention in Des Moines declared that, while Iowa agriculture remained highly developed, manufacturing hadn't followed. This situation was detrimental for farmers when railroad freight rates remained monopolistically unregulated and uncontrollably high.

Before year's end, Warren County farmers took action. They incorporated an entity known as the Warren County Manufacturing Society with Joel Jacoby as their champion. Incorporation meant funds solicited for a defined purpose and entrusted to a board of directors held the promise for a return on investment for those taking risk. While Jacoby was currently running a small 8x12 foot manufacturing business, this endeavor was for something much larger and more consequential.

It is unclear if sufficient funds were raised for a two-story 30x150 structure but Jacoby did expand his operation. In the spring of 1875, Indianola Agricultural Works began producing farm and spring wagons, buggies of every description, double and single cultivators, and harrows of all kinds.

With newspaper advertisements listing everything they produced, a message at the bottom in much smaller font spoke to the uneasiness of taking this large leap:

"Hoping that I may receive a liberal patronage as I have incurred a large expense in fitting up for the good of the public—Joel Jacoby."

A year later, Jacoby sold the agricultural works to an experienced Des Moines firm and not a ripple of discontent found its way to the printed page. It can be assumed the investors were well-satisfied.

Joel Jacoby was looking ahead—Indianola needed a new hotel. The *Indianola-Tribune* wrote in January 1876: "Mr Joel Jacoby, who is always alive to any and all kinds of improvement is taking the lead in passing a subscription paper for stock and is succeeding finely."

The Central House block, northeast side of The Square, abutting Jacoby's Block, stands today. Built at the same time, both are fine examples of historically significant architecture and reminders of Joel Jacoby's ability to embolden a community.

However, this enterprising life-force wasn't done. In 1882, he built a canning factory for anything in season (corn, beans, tomatoes). Located near the railroad tracks north of Simpson's Smith Chapel, the factory employed both men and women.

Unfortunately, Joel Jacoby's life ended on December 26, 1886. After smashing several fingers taking down a buggy hood, he succumbed slowly over a six-months to an infection gone awry. Jacoby was only fifty-nine years old and access to an antibiotic was sixty years into the future. Many accolades accompanied this early pioneer to the Indianola IOOF Cemetery because "the better elements predominated in his nature."

Indianola gladly followed this Pied Piper of community enhancement. **Begging The Question**, who do we follow today?

FINDING HOPE IN
BLURRING BOUNDARIES

Most Iowa counties, excluding those edging the borders, have squarish shapes. Warren County is an exception with its raggedy upper right corner. **Begging The Question**, what happened?

On January 13th 1846, when Iowa's legislative body established Warren County's boundaries along with our Polk, Dallas, and Madison neighbors, our county had a normal squarish silhouette. However, four days later a supplemental act expanded Polk County into Warren's upper tier, extracting a swath or strip spanning the entire length of our shared border.

This aggressive and unneighborly grab was the stealthy undertaking of fledging Fort Des Moines. Stealing "The Strip" placed them at the center of Polk County, which was advantageous for deciding the location of the coveted county courthouse. With other communities vying for the honor, ravaging Warren County got Fort Des Moines what they wanted and everyone moved on to other matters.

Six years later, Representative P Gad Bryan of Indianola introduced petitions and legislation to reclaim The Strip during Iowa's 4th General Assembly. His bill sailed through the House but hit rough waters in the Senate.

Senator Andrew Hull of Polk County, owning a farm north of the Des Moines River inside Warren's original outline, didn't favor the restoration. It legislated him out of office.

Representative Bryan understood the man's dilemma and sought a compromise by blurring boundaries. On January 14th 1853, The Strip was returned to Warren County with a raggedy northeast corner following the zigzagging of the

Des Moines River. The solution left Hull's elected position secure with his property inside Polk County.

Described later in life as having a "gentile and old-fashioned hospitality that is quite attractive," Peter Gad Bryan was born in Ohio and a graduate of Indiana's Wabash Medical College. Traveling here in 1850 made him an early settler. After deciding to read for the law, he was admitted into the bar in 1852 and practiced both medicine and law before dropping doctoring because "my patients all died."

A lifelong Democrat, P Gad didn't vote for Republican candidate Abraham Lincoln in the 1860 presidential election. However, the following year he organized a cavalry unit at his expense to defend our government's integrity against a Confederate rebellion.

Running for a Congressional seat in 1868, P Gad Bryan's Republican opponent was on the same ticket as presidential candidate Ulysses S Grant. With postwar rancor for the South's reconstruction running rampant, P Gad's debate arguments landed weak and "with the air of a man who knows he's in the wrong." He lost by a wide margin.

Moving to Des Moines in 1875, P Gad regularly returned to Indianola for courtroom appearances and to visit family and friends. When asked to run for Congress again, he replied, "No gentlemen, no more Congress in me."

Unlike the gentle meandering of the Des Moines River in our raggedy northeast corner, Peter Gad Bryan experienced the **Hard Edges** of party politics. His early success with compromise by blurring boundaries to find bipartisan solutions may have gotten lost and forgotten but it's there for us to coax and nurture again.

BEING COMFORTABLE AND GOOD WORKING ORDER

Addressing the **Hard Edges** of constipation, Dr Pierce's Pleasant Pellets not only cured the consequences but invigorated the stomach and liver for return to good working order. These sugar-coated purgative pellets provided a natural cure for biliousness, indigestion, stomach pain, and excessive flatulence.

Advertised in Indianola newspapers beginning in the early 1870s, the wondrous morsels also assisted with the actions of Dr Pierce's Golden Medical Discovery. This licorice-flavored tonic resolved a range of issues, from dizziness and liver trouble to eczema and skin eruptions. Discovery, as it was called, bathed the blood in a refreshing mixture of natural ingredients, allowing the "vital fires of the body to burn brighter."

Dr Ray Vaughn Pierce, creator of these miraculous remedies, studied medicine and graduated from an eclectic medical college in the 1860s. His training followed a branch of medicine using natural ingredients as opposed to noxious mixtures and invasive treatments. While he practiced for only a short time, his entrepreneurial skills and desire to help thousands lured him into manufacturing.

Pierce built a mega-size facility in Buffalo, New York. His products were dispensed by drugstores nationwide, including those in Warren County. Advertisements for his prescriptions headlined a condition (Dizziness and Consumption) or enticed with a catchy phrase (Save the Child, Women Wonder Why, and Why Have Nerves).

In keeping with his eclectic training, Dr Pierce published a 1008-page tome entitled *Common Sense Medical Advisor* which stressed the importance of nutrition, hygiene, water purity, and exercise. He also advised that when the heart is oppressed and movement slows due to a languishing blood flow "in these moments alcohol cheers."

With his remedies regularly ingested by Warren County residents, Pierce's preparations were analyzed in 1893 and published along with five thousand others in a formulary for druggists. In addition to honey and lactucarium (wild lettuce), Dr Pierce's Discovery was found to be 64% alcohol with a tincture of opium.

When the formulary was updated in 1900, the editors included an affidavit from Dr Pierce proclaiming, "There is not at the present time, nor has there ever been, any alcohol, opium, choral, cocaine or other narcotic used as ingredient." Immediately following, the editors explained there must have been an error during analysis or imperfect samples were analyzed.

However, significant and long-lasting damage had been done. Advertisements for Pierce's products now included statements regarding their purity: "absolutely a temperance medicine," and "without alcohol and free of opium, cocaine and other narcotics."

In 1903, the *Ladies Home Journal* published the inaccurate ingredient information and labeled Pierce a quack. Dr Ray Vaughn Pierce sued the magazine, proved his products didn't contain alcohol and narcotics, and was awarded $16,000 ($600,000 today).

Despite the long-ago vindication, blogs and online articles today use the erroneous information and tag Dr Pierce a quack. The reason is clear. It's easier to grab hold of juicy information, cling tight, and never listen again.

Back in the day, Warren County residents didn't succumb to these **Shenanigans**. Dr Pierce's herbal remedies remained on drugstore shelves into the 1940s.

CLEAR THINKING
WITHOUT SHENANIGANS

Shenanigans is a curious word unearthed during California's 1855 Gold Rush. Rooted in behavior that's devious, underhanded, and tricky, this is a complimentary reference to the Reeves family, who were driven from Warren County seven years before the word was coined.

George and Elizabeth Reeves married when she was twelve and the couple had fourteen children. Originally from Grayson County, Virginia, the family's pioneer thieving days, first in Illinois and then Iowa, are difficult to verify since they operated before the arrival of newspapers and court systems. Their notoriety was documented years later based on recollections from feeble minds entangled by personal opinion.

The George Reeves family gang arrived in Warren County during the fall of 1845, before the Sac and Fox tribes had completely departed. As a result of their thieving, burgling, and possibly rustling activities, the family was looking for a fresh start after being escorted out of Illinois by a three-hundred-member posse representing multiple counties.

Mother Elizabeth was described as the "ruling spirit of the family and its evil genius" by Spencer Ellsworth in his 1880 publication *Record of Olden Time: Fifty Years On The Prairie*. Teaching her boys to pillage and plunder, this model of motherhood was likely transferring the survival skills she learned during an abbreviated and dysfunctional upbringing.

Establishing a home base in Linn Grove (between Cummings and Norwalk), it took three years of desperado-type activities and petty crimes coupled with emerging horse-rustling rumors for things to escalate and become a slippery slope for the Reeves. The tipping point arrived after eldest son Cameron shot James Phipps, who survived although some recollections wrongfully say he was killed.

Following the same process as Illinois, a large vigilante group from Polk, Warren, and Madison counties gathered on horseback and on foot (booted and barefoot). Subduing the Linn Grove sheriff from issuing an arrest warrant against their anticipated actions, this free-roaming lawless horde began rounding up the Reeves. Surrounding and containing those at the Linn Grove homestead, they found those ensconced at a Fort Des Moines bar. They were also able to track down Cameron after his escape from the Osceola jail. The vigilantes escorted the entire clan west into Adair County and then they were carefully monitored before the Reeves family finally crossing Iowa's border into Missouri.

Shenanigans by the Reeves then ceased, which somewhat correlates with the 1852 passing of father George. Miraculously, remaining family members became productive members of fledging Omaha, Nebraska. Cameron was elected sheriff, brothers Preston and Jesse attained wealth and respect, and sister Sophronia married Omaha's founder AD Jones.

Most surprising, mother Elizabeth became the first woman physician in Nebraska. Ministering to the less fortunate using the self-taught skills acquired over years of mending family members, she passed into eternity at ninety-three years of age. Her 1892 obituary mentioned leaving "many friends, especially among the poorer classes, to mourn her death."

Given the Reeves massive transformation, asking each of us to take a **Clean Slate** fresh look at ourselves and become a better persons seems a comparatively small ask.

Clean Slate of Acknowledgments

I want to thank Amy Duncan, editor and owner of the online *Indianola Independent-Advocate*, for publishing "The Unbroken Line of Pondering." While I was surprised to find my monthly column under the opinion tab, it made the writing more creative, exploratory, and considerably more fun.

Secondly, many thanks to all the hard-working individuals, past and present, at the Warren County Historical Society & Museum. Their foresight bringing our county's old newspapers online attached to a strong search engine enabled finding the perspectives and circumstances swirling around these glimpses from the past. This treasure trove of history is available to anyone, anytime, and from anywhere (warren.advantage-preservation.com).

I want to thank my Writers' Group: Linda Railey, Susan Hoffert, and Susan Raye. They read all pieces and made countless suggestions. We are sisters in our hearts and remain indebted to our mentor Mary Kay Shanley. Her lessons continue guiding "our writerly selves."

Thank you to my readers for letting me know when I got it exactly right. They also alleviated my greatest fear: "Is anyone reading my stuff?"

I am grateful to Kathy Magruder, owner of Pageturners on The Square's southeast corner. Her steady voice provided the calm and resolve to enter the world of self-publishing and ensure this book was available to independent bookstores.

Many thanks to Sandy for never questioning all my printing, trashed drafts, and countless hours researching, writing, and editing.

Lastly, thank you for purchasing these glimpses of Warren County, Iowa. It's been a joy discovering and sharing lost history. Hope is a natural outcome from studying the past because, as perspective is altered, understanding comes closer.

About the Author

Elodie lives in Indianola, county seat for Warren County, Iowa, with her husband Sandy and their cat Ricky. After retiring from a career in healthcare, she took a writing class and needed a project. While her first work of historical fiction remains unpublished, there's hope and wherewithal this publication provides the impetus to push forward and share an unbelievably great story.

Enjoying family, friends, community, gardening, and reading a variety of genres, Elodie and Sandy enjoy traveling, which they have been doing for over forty years. Doing their own research and believing the GPS is one of the most significant innovations in their lifetime, getting serendipitously lost remains a travel passion.

Serving on a variety of committees, organizations, and projects, Elodie is beginning her second decade as a Medicare volunteer counselor for the Iowa SHIIP/SMP program. She can be reached regarding this publication at elodie3opstad@gmail.com.

Printed in the USA
CPSIA information can be obtained
at www.ICGtesting.com
LVHW031609071224
798390LV00013B/887

* 9 7 9 8 2 1 8 4 8 0 2 8 8 *